JACK DANIEL'S
Hometown Celebration
COOKBOOK
VOLUME II

COME VISIT US

PAT MITCHAMORE

with recipes edited by

LYNNE TOLLEY

Rutledge Hill Press

Published in Nashville, Tennessee, by Rutledge Hill Press, Inc., 513 Third Avenue South, Nashville, Tennessee 37210

Photographs on pages 13, 20 (right), 25, 51 (left and right), 62 (all), 63, 85, 99, 111, 123, 126, 137, 145, 153 (left and right), 165, 173, and 181 by Hope Powell and reprinted by permission.

Photographs on pages 14, 23, 38, 44, 54, 67, 80, 87, 90, 108, 129 (left and right), 143 and 175 copyright by Junebug Clark and reprinted by permission.

Photographs on pages 16, 28, 42, 58, 76, 88, 102, 114, and 148 by Mike Rutherford and reprinted by permission.

Photographs on pages 20 (left), 79, 93 (left), and 177 by Mark Neal and reprinted by permission.

Photographs on pages 35 and 69 by Pat Mitchamore and reprinted by permission.

Photograph on page 46 by Diane Overstreet and reprinted by permission.

Photographs on pages 93 (right) and 168 by Slick Lawson and reprinted by permission.

Photograph on page 132 courtesy of International Apple Institute and reprinted by permission.

Photograph on page 160 copyright by Robin Hood and reprinted by permission.

Food styling for jacket photograph by Mary Ann Fowlkes

Jacket and text design by Harriette Bateman

Typography by Bailey Typography, Nashville, Tennessee

Printed in the United States of America by R. R. Donnelley and Sons

Library of Congress Cataloging-in-Publication Data

Mitchamore, Pat, 1934-
   Jack Daniel's hometown celebration cookbook, volume 2 / Pat Mitchamore : with recipes edited by Lynne Tolley.
      p.   cm.
   Includes index.
   ISBN 1-55853-085-1
   1. Cookery (Whiskey) I. Tolley, Lynne, 1950- . II. Title.
TX726.M57 1990   90-8964
641.6′25—dc20   CIP

      1 2 3 4 5 6 7 8 9 — 97 96 95 94 93 92 91 90

CONTENTS

▪ INTRODUCTION ▪

After writing *Jack Daniel's The Spirit of Tennessee Cookbook*, we shared many conversations about food, its preparation and presentation, and what certain dishes mean to people. We received letters with recipes and stories about those recipes. The history of family dishes, the traditions and memories associated with these dishes, and the joy in preparing an old family dish were what prompted this book.

Fascination with food goes far beyond our creature needs and comforts. Our feelings about a certain dish prepared a certain way may be sparked by remembering the hospitality of a person or by a traditional celebration. Another dish might bring to mind moments lost in the cluttered attic of our minds where days-past hover, ready to be rediscovered. Food is almost always connected with special occasions and celebrations, tantalizing our senses and tugging at our hearts as we remember our family, our friends, our life, and our hometown.

The place we call our hometown is usually where childhood was spent, the time in our life when things were simple, uncluttered, and uncomplicated. We were cared for by loving people, and the world lay waiting to be remade in the optimism of childhood and youth. When we grew up, the freedom of childhood stayed in childhood; living and making a living became the order of the day. Thus, when anything takes us back to that more simple time, we are reminded of our hometown.

Because childhood was simple, so were our celebrations: making the little league team, getting a new tooth, birthday parties, or campfire cookouts. We enjoyed the homecoming queen's coronation, slumber parties, and graduation. These were not big celebrations and they were not celebrated by everyone in town, at least not at the same time. Rather they were *our* events in *our* home and in *our* town.

Hometown celebrations have enriched our lives, nourished our sense of place and self-esteem, and nurtured our feelings of security. The foods that were served on these simple occasions still mean something to us. Mom made our favorite cake if we won the spelling bee. She made Dad's favorite apple pie to celebrate his return from a week away from home. Grandma made our favorite doughnuts for breakfast every time we spent the night at her house. Our favorite cookies were standard for such events as learning to swim, a piano recital, or a homeroom party. They said, "This is special, something to celebrate." Unlike Mardi Gras, Christmas, or Easter, which everyone everywhere celebrated, these were happenings about us and for us and our achievements—personal celebrations.

We now re-create these special celebrations for our children and grandchildren. Once again, in the preparation and serving of long-time favorite dishes, we make hometown celebrations special.

That is what this book is about: foods that have been special to a lot of people. Some of these recipes have been in families for a hundred years, eaten and enjoyed at many celebrations and occasions. Some of the family members are gone, but they are remembered when the aroma of a cake, hot bread, or pot roast wafts through our kitchens. We laugh when we eat the "Tater Piggies" we used to eat at schoolgirl slumber parties. We have a sense of being loved when we smell the aroma of "Celebration Bread" or "Chuck Wagon Cobbler." We are engulfed with memories of youth when we eat "Texas Sheet Cake" that we took to every pot luck church social. The taste of "Spare Ribs Delicious" or "Joy Cake" reminds us of Dad and the things that Mama cooked just to please him if he worked late or had been away.

It was fun putting this cookbook together—fun for us and fun for those who remembered why their recipes were special to them. We think it will be fun for you to try them. Maybe you will add them to your roster for home celebrations and special occasions. We hope so!

Hometown here is represented by Lynchburg, Tennessee. In many ways, Lynchburg is the quintessential representation of hometowns everywhere. It is probably the most recognizable small town in America because of the advertising of Jack Daniel's Whiskey. Folk here are down-to-earth, salt of the earth, good neighbors, and family people. They are hospitable and loving . . . and great cooks.

Because of this, we are featuring a lot of those who call Lynchburg their hometown. They are hosts to about 250,000 visitors to the Jack Daniel Distillery every year, and they extend an invitation for you to come see them and their hometown in the near future. When you arrive, you can enjoy a great tour—free— of the distillery, which is on the National Register of Historic Places; shop on the town square; and, if you make reservations, have lunch with Lynne at Miss Bobo's Boarding House. Some of Lynchburg's celebrations are pictured here. But even if you miss one of the big events, Lynchburg will do its best to make you welcome. Y'all come!

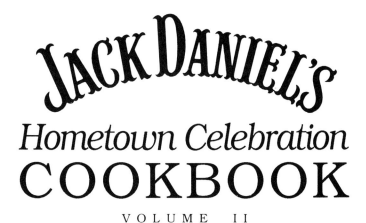

JACK DANIEL'S

Hometown Celebration

COOKBOOK

VOLUME II

· DRINKS ·

The right drink puts you into the spirit of an occasion. Trying new combinations of ingredients can bring about a delightful discovery of new tastes. For instance, it is surprising that cream blends beautifully with so many flavorings, or that citrus juices can serve as a base for so many punches. Colas and other sparkling beverages tickle our taste buds.

This chapter includes a number of favorite drinks created both by professional bartenders and by home bartenders for their guests. Many include Lynchburg's hometown product, Jack Daniel's Whiskey. Other chapters show that some cooks use it to flavor cakes, sauces, and marinades, but far and away the best way to use it is in a drink. This collection includes many new ways of using an old favorite.

· *Hot Candied Apple Punch* ·

This is an excellent hot drink that adults and children both can drink. A real plus—the aroma drifts through the whole house and smells so good!

2 gallons apple cider or apple juice
1 cup cinnamon red hot candies

Place apple cider in large 32-cup percolator (use percolator only). Place candies in coffee basket. Perk as for coffee. Delicious . . . and it smells good, too.

Makes 32 cups.

• *Wassail* •

This is our traditional Christmas Eve drink.

2 tablespoons whole allspice
16 whole cloves
1 cinnamon stick
1 gallon apple cider
1½ cups sugar

Tie spices in a cheesecloth square. Drop into hot, simmering cider. Stir in sugar; simmer for 30 minutes . . . do not boil.
Makes 20 servings.

Thelma Grisham

• *Tennessee Spice Tea* •

1 cup sugar-free powdered ice tea mix with lemon
½ cup powdered orange drink
½ teaspoon cinnamon
½ teaspoon nutmeg
Jack Daniel's Whiskey
Lemon slice

Mix dry ingredients well; store in airtight container. To make 1 drink: Mix 1 heaping teaspoon dry ingredients with 1 cup hot water and 1 ounce Jack Daniel's Whiskey. Garnish with lemon slice. Serve in a mug during the winter and over ice during the summer.

John Long

• *Jack Daniel's Last Kick* •

1 part Jack Daniel's Whiskey
3 parts pink grapefruit juice
Maraschino cherry

Combine Jack Daniel's Whiskey and pink grapefruit juice. Pour over ice; garnish with maraschino cherry. Makes 1 serving.

Melody Ray

The next eight recipes were created by bartenders in Memphis for a drink contest during the Beale Street Jazz Festival in 1988.

• *Mockingbird Blossom* •

Several strawberries or blackberries
1½ ounces Jack Daniel's Whiskey
Dash of bitters
7-Up
1 lemon twist
Splash of Irish whiskey

Mash berries; combine with Jack Daniel's Whiskey and bitters over crushed ice in a tall glass. Fill with 7-Up. Garnish with a lemon twist; top with a splash of Irish whiskey.
Makes 1 serving.

Jeff Dlugach

▪ *Jackie Blue* ▪

1¼ ounces Jack Daniel's Whiskey
¾ ounce blueberry schnapps
4 ounces bottled sweet & sour mix
2 ounces 7-Up

Stir all ingredients with cracked ice in a tall glass.
Makes 1 serving.

David Thomas

▪ *Jack 340* ▪

2 ounces Jack Daniel's Whiskey
2 ounces peach brandy
3 ounces bottled sweet & sour mix
Ginger ale

Combine ingredients and serve over cracked ice.
Makes 1 serving.

Butch Jordan

▪ *Sassy Jack* ▪

¾ ounce Jack Daniel's Whiskey
3 ounces apple juice
1 sassafras stick

Combine Jack Daniel's Whiskey and apple juice over ice
in an old-fashioned glass. Garnish with sassafras
stick.
Makes 1 serving.

Eddie King

▪ *Apple Jack* ▪

1½ ounces Jack Daniel's Whiskey
1½ ounces apple juice
1 ounce orange juice
¾ ounce honey

Shake all ingredients in cocktail shaker filled with ice.
Strain into a stemmed glass.
Makes 1 serving.

Carolyn Priori

▪ *Black Eye* ▪

1¼ ounces Jack Daniel's Whiskey
¼ ounce blackberry brandy
¼ ounce bottled sweet & sour mix
Lemon wedge
Splash of club soda

Combine first three ingredients in a glass. Squeeze
lemon wedge in glass and drop in. Add ice cubes and a
splash of club soda.
Makes 1 serving.

John Ross/Jim Hooper

Billy Jack

¾ ounce Jack Daniel's Whiskey
¾ ounce Triple Sec
¾ ounce Amaretto
 Bottled sweet & sour mix
 Splash of Grenadine

Combine first three ingredients in a tall glass. Add ice cubes and fill glass with sweet and sour mix. Stir; top with a splash of Grenadine.
 Makes 1 serving.

Billy Stephenson

Motone

1 ounce Jack Daniel's Whiskey
½ ounce blueberry brandy
3 parts 7-Up
 Limes

Stir together Jack Daniel's Whiskey and brandy in a tall glass. Add ice cubes and top with 7-Up. Garnish with a lime wedge or slice.
 Makes 1 serving.

Sam Merriweather

Tennessee Tea

1 part Jack Daniel's Whiskey
½ part Amaretto
3 parts pineapple juice
 Splash of Coke®

Combine all ingredients over ice.
 Makes 1 serving.

Dandelion Wine

Old-fashioned as it may be, homemade wine is still in fashion in rural areas all over the country. Old family recipes abound and following are two very good ones. These came to me from a friend and we love them. They are great conversational drinks—besides being just plain good!

1 quart boiling water
1 quart dandelion flowers
3 quarts cold water
4 pounds sugar
 Juice from 2 freshly squeezed lemons

In large crock or stone jar, pour boiling water over the flowers. Let stand overnight. Strain, reserving liquid. Add cold water to liquid. Add sugar and lemon juice. Store in a covered stone jar for 6 weeks. Bottle and cork or place in a glass gallon jug and cap.
 Makes 1 gallon.

Family Reunions

Bill and Mary Edde and Clarence Rolman

For more than twenty years Bill and Mary Edde have run the Lynchburg Auto Parts store on the town square. They know just about everybody in these parts because this is their hometown. Occupying a corner just across from the office of *The Moore County News*, they keep up with what is going on in town.

Clarence and Elvie Rolman, Mary's parents, grew up on farms in the area. When Clarence was a youngster, moonshiners were as prevalent as the hills they lived on. Everyone kept a little "shine" for celebrations and for medicinal purposes. When prohibition closed down all the legal stills (such as Jack Daniel's), country folk went to "farming in the woods." Clarence admits he did a little moonshining, and made enough money to buy a little farm and marry his sweetheart, Elvie.

They were married for more than sixty years and have raised a fine family. Clarence started to work for the Jack Daniel Distillery in 1938. When he retired, he became a tour guide at the Welcome Center. Later the distillery sent him out to meet consumers all over the country, sort of an ambassador from Lynchburg. He and Elvie traveled all over the United States, Canada, Australia, New Zealand, and the United Kingdom. They finally stopped traveling in 1983 when Elvie became ill.

Occasions to celebrate were their homecomings back to Tennessee, the farm, and their family. Big Sunday dinners, and backyard picnics were planned so that their three children, the grandchildren, and the great-grandchildren could welcome them home and hear about the most recent trip.

Clarence has a lot of stories about his journeys, but his favorites are the ones he tells about Lynchburg and the Jack Daniel Distillery. He recalls that he has done just about every job there was to do at the distillery except one: whiskey taster. The reason, he says, is that a whiskey taster can never swallow the Jack Daniel's while tasting. And he knew that if he got that Jack Daniel's in his mouth, there was no way on earth that he was going to spit it out.

Square dancing is great fun. Toes tap, skirts swirl, and partners swing as the caller gathers squares to the beat of the music. Not many hometowns have a gazebo, but this day, while the Mr. Jack Daniel's Original Silver Cornet Band was on tour, these dancers made good use of the empty gazebo in Lynchburg.

■ *Rhubarb Wine* ■

16 pounds rhubarb
6 lemons, cut into wedges
6 oranges, cut into wedges
4 cups raisins
20 quarts water
16 pounds sugar

Mash rhubarb and place with fruit in a stone jar. Add water; let stand for 9 days. Strain; discard rhubarb and fruit; reserve liquid. Add sugar to liquid. Cover, stir once or twice a day. Let stand for at least 6 weeks. Strain, skim well and bottle.
Makes 20 quarts.

■ *Whiskey Sour Punch* ■

1 12-ounce can frozen orange juice
1 12-ounce can frozen lemonade
1 20-ounce can pineapple juice
1 liter Jack Daniel's Whiskey
1 liter ginger ale

In large crock or container, dilute frozen juices together using amount of water stated on cans. Add pineapple juice and stir well. Chill until ready to serve. Pour into punch bowl; add Jack Daniel's Whiskey and ginger ale.
Makes 25 servings.

■ *The Liberty* ■

1 ounce Jack Daniel's Whiskey
½ ounce Southern Comfort
1 ounce dry white vermouth
½ ounce Rose's lime juice
Maraschino cherry

Combine first 4 ingredients with ice; shake and strain into cocktail glass. Decorate with maraschino cherry. Makes 1 drink.

14

▪ *C. Rolman's Year-round Toddy* ▪

Clarence Rolman attributes his long healthy life to using this recipe.

Jack Daniel's Whiskey
Honey

In a 750ml bottle leave two inches of Jack Daniel's Whiskey. Fill the remainder of the bottle with honey. Shake to mix. Take a swig when you feel a cold coming on or you feel a little under the weather or for reasons unknown. You're sure to feel better and will be able to think up a good reason for needing another sip of toddy! Guaranteed good for what ails you!

▪ *La Creme Damage* ▪

My wife and I were of the opinion that Jack Daniel's Whiskey could not and should not be mixed with anything as this would spoil the excellent flavor of this fine sipping whiskey. However, purely by accident, we have found Jack Daniel's Whiskey and a nice helping of Breyer's Vanilla Bean Ice Cream is the perfect adult milkshake. We have named our concoction "La Creme Damage." Be cautious. This is an extremely smooth drink.

Breyer's Vanilla Bean Ice Cream
Jack Daniel's Whiskey

In a tumbler, mix to taste Breyer's Vanilla Bean Ice Cream and Jack Daniel's Whiskey. Lay back and enjoy!
Makes 1 drink.

Kenneth B. Holliday

▪ *The South Sun* ▪

1 ounce Jack Daniel's Whiskey
1½ ounces Southern Comfort
2½ ounces orange juice
2 dashes Grenadine
1 dash tangerine liqueur
Orange peel

Shake all ingredients over ice and serve in a large cocktail glass garnished with orange peel.
Makes 1 drink.

Jean-Jacques Charbonnier

▪ *The President* ▪

1 ounce Jack Daniel's Whiskey
2½ ounces heavy cream
1 ounce banana liqueur
½ ounce coffee liqueur
Powdered or flaked chocolate

Shake first 4 ingredients over ice and serve in cocktail glass. Sprinkle a little powdered or flaked chocolate on top.
Makes 1 drink.

Bob Burton

15

· APPETIZERS ·

Sometimes appetizers are so good that you can make a meal out of them. In truth, they are designed to whet our appetites—or, as the word implies, tease our appetites—for what is to come. Fast foods, snack foods, and finger foods are favorites of everyone. Dips, chips, seafood, chicken, meatballs, cheese and spreads are all eaten at the beginning of meals. Whatever tastes good is good as an appetizer. The trick is to make appetizers in small portions so that when the main event happens, everyone is still hungry enough to enjoy it.

· *Cheesy Sesame Popcorn* ·

2 quarts popped popcorn
2 tablespoons butter, melted
2 tablespoons grated Parmesan
  cheese or Romano cheese
2 teaspoons sesame seed
¼ teaspoon celery salt, optional

Keep popcorn warm. Combine remaining ingredients; drizzle over popcorn. Stir or shake till evenly coated. Makes 2 quarts.

Susan Byars

• *Favorite Caramel Corn* •

3¾ quarts popped corn (about 15 cups)
2 cups packed brown sugar
2 sticks butter
½ cup light corn syrup
½ teaspoon salt
1 teaspoon baking soda

Preheat oven to 200°. Divide popped corn between two 13x9x2-inch baking pans. Combine sugar, butter, corn syrup and salt in a heavy saucepan. Cook, stirring occasionally, until bubbly around the edges. Continue cooking over medium heat 5 minutes more. Remove from heat. Stir in soda. Pour over popcorn; gently stir to coat evenly. Bake for 1 hour; stir every 15 minutes.
Makes 3¾ quarts.

Lynne Findley

• *Pigs-In-A-Blanket* •

1 package hot dogs
Cheese
Bacon

Slit hot dogs down sides without going through the ends or other side. Gently press cheese into cavity (like filling a little boat). Wrap with half a slice of bacon; secure with a toothpick. Place on baking sheet; broil for a few minutes. Watch carefully until cheese is melted and bacon is crisp. This is especially good served as a meal with baked beans, bread and butter.
Makes 8 to 10 servings.

• *Tater Piggies* •

When I was a girl, Tater Piggies were a favorite when we had slumber parties. There weren't that many snack foods on the market then, and special dishes like "pigs-in-a-blanket" and Tater Piggies were fixed for these fun and casual parties. They were inexpensive, easy and had names that seemed to fit our age and the event.

2 cups cooked mashed potatoes
8 hot dogs, cut in half crosswise
½ cup cornflake crumbs
½ cup dark corn syrup
1 2½-ounce can French-fried onion rings

Preheat oven to 350°. Using hands, press the mashed potatoes around the hot dog halves to cover. Roll in cornflake crumbs; place in an 8-inch square baking pan. Drizzle syrup on top; cover with onion rings. Bake, uncovered, for 20 to 25 minutes—they should be well browned and crisp.
Makes 16 servings.

▪ *Bacon-Wrapped Piggies* ▪

When my husband and I lived in California, I gave a birthday party for him. One of the ladies invited to the party gave me this recipe. Each time I have served it everyone asks for the recipe. It is the perfect answer for entertaining because it is so quick and easy . . . and sure to please.

2 packages sausage links
1 pound bacon
1 1-pound box brown sugar

Preheat oven to 325°. Remove casing from sausage links. Cut each sausage and bacon slice in thirds and wrap bacon around pieces; secure with a toothpick. Place in a 13x9x2-inch baking pan. Pour the brown sugar evenly over the sausage. Bake for 1 hour; remove and serve.
Makes 32 servings.

Tina Terry

▪ *Spinach Tidbits* ▪

4 tablespoons butter
3 eggs
1 cup all-purpose flour
1 cup milk
1 teaspoon salt
1 teaspoon baking powder
1 pound sharp cheddar cheese, grated
1 onion, grated
2 10-ounce packages frozen spinach, thawed and drained

Preheat oven to 350°. Melt butter in a 13x9x2-inch pan. In mixing bowl, beat eggs; add flour, milk, salt and baking powder. Mix well. Add grated cheese, onion and spinach. Pour over melted butter in pan; bake for 35 minutes. Cool and cut into desired shapes. Serve as hors d'oeuvres.
Makes 2 dozen.

▪ *Cheesy Chicken* ▪

4 pounds chicken wings
1 cup grated Parmesan-Romano cheese
2 tablespoons minced parsley
1 tablespoon oregano
2 teaspoons paprika
1 teaspoon salt
½ teaspoon freshly cracked pepper

Preheat oven to 350°. Cut each chicken wing into three sections at joints. Discard pointed ends. Place remaining ingredients into a large zipper-type plastic bag. Drop chicken pieces, a few at a time, into bag and shake, coating each wing carefully with the cheese mixture. Place on a well-greased baking sheet; bake for 1 hour. Serve immediately. *Note:* These can be prepared ahead of time and baked just before the party. Cover baking sheets and chill until ready to bake.
Makes about 24 appetizers.

19

▪ *Favorite Shrimp Mold* ▪

1½ tablespoons gelatin
¼ cup cold water
2 cups diced, cooked shrimp
2 hard-boiled eggs, grated
1 medium onion, chopped
1½ cups mayonnaise
   Crackers

Soften gelatin in cold water. Heat on low for several minutes until dissolved. Combine gelatin mixture with remaining ingredients, except crackers. Pour into oiled mold. Chill until firm. Unmold and serve with crackers.
   Makes 12 servings.

Betty J. Grimm

▪ *Veggie Bars* ▪

2 packages crescent roll dough
2 8-ounce packages cream cheese, softened
1 cup mayonnaise
1 package ranch salad dressing mix
   Chopped vegetables

Cover bottom of pan with flat pieces of dough. Bake according to directions on can. Let cool. Combine cream cheese, mayonnaise and salad dressing mix. Spread mixture over rolls. Top with finely chopped broccoli, cauliflower, red pepper, green onion, finely grated carrots, sliced mushrooms and black olives. Chill. Cut into squares.
   Makes 12 to 16 servings.

Fran Houser

Football victories and homecoming queen coronations are happy events in every hometown. The next day there will be country ham and biscuits for breakfast as the family celebrates the touchdowns of the night before and a cake for dinner to match the splendor of the queen's coronation.

Fried Cheese Wedges with Special Tomato Sauce ■

1 pound Monterey Jack or cheddar
cheese (in brick form)
1 cup fine dry bread crumbs
1 cup toasted wheat germ
¼ teaspoon ground red pepper
1 tablespoon butter
1 8-ounce can tomato sauce
1 2-ounce can mushroom stems
and pieces, drained and chopped
½ teaspoon crushed dried basil
½ teaspoon crushed dried oregano
4 eggs, beaten
Vegetable oil
Cherry tomatoes, halved; whole
sweet pickles; boiled whole new
potatoes

Cut cheese into 2x1½x¾-inch rectangles, then cut each rectangle into 2 wedges. Cover and chill in the refrigerator. In a small mixing bowl, stir together bread crumbs, wheat germ and ground red pepper; set aside. Melt butter in saucepan. Stir in tomato sauce, mushrooms, basil and oregano. Bring to a boil; reduce heat. Simmer, uncovered, about 5 minutes, stirring occasionally. Cover and keep warm while preparing cheese. Dip the chilled cheese wedges into beaten egg to coat evenly, then roll in bread crumb mixture. Dip wedges into egg again and roll again in crumb mixture. In a 3-quart saucepan or a deep-fat fryer heat 3 inches of oil to 375°. Fry cheese wedges, a few at a time, in hot oil for 30 to 60 seconds or until golden brown on all sides. Remove fried cheese and drain on paper towels. Keep warm in a 250° oven while frying remaining cheese. Serve warm with tomato-mushroom sauce. If desired, accompany with cherry tomatoes, sweet pickles and new potatoes.

Makes about 20 cheese wedges.

■ Bambini ■

This is a great party appetizer. I serve it a lot around Christmas. Leftover bambinis are also good for breakfast the next morning.

1 cup ricotta cheese
½ cup grated Mozzarella cheese
¼ cup Parmesan cheese
1 10-ounce package large flaky
refrigerator biscuits
20 very thin slices pepperoni

Preheat oven to 350°. Combine ricotta, Mozzarella and Parmesan cheese in a small bowl; mix well. Halve each biscuit horizontally, forming 20 thin biscuits. Gently shape one piece of dough into a 2x4-inch oval. Place a slice of pepperoni slightly off center on dough. Top with about 1 level tablespoon of cheese mixture. Moisten edges; fold dough over to enclose filling, pinching edges carefully to seal. Transfer to a lightly greased cookie sheet. Bake for 20 minutes until golden brown. Serve warm.

Makes 20 appetizers.

∎ *Stuffed Mushrooms* ∎

12 mushrooms
1 stick butter or margarine, divided
3 tablespoons chopped green peppers
3 tablespoons chopped onions
1½ cups fresh bread cubes
Salt and pepper to taste

Preheat oven to 350°. Wipe mushrooms with damp cloth. Remove stems, leaving caps intact. Chop stems. Sauté caps in 3 tablespoons butter; set aside. Sauté stems, peppers and onion in remaining butter for 5 minutes. Add bread cubes and seasonings. Stuff each cap with mixture. Place on greased baking pan. Bake for 10 minutes.

Makes 4 servings.

Renate Stone

∎ *Salmon Ball* ∎

1 15-ounce can skinless and boneless salmon
1 8-ounce package cream cheese, softened
1 teaspoon lemon juice
2 teaspoons grated onion or more
1 teaspoon prepared horseradish
¼ teaspoon salt
¼ teaspoon liquid smoke
½ cup chopped pecans
3 tablespoons snipped fresh parsley or parsley flakes
Crackers

Drain salmon. Combine salmon, cream cheese, lemon juice, onion, horseradish, salt and liquid smoke. Mix thoroughly and chill overnight. Combine pecans and parsley. Shape salmon mixture into a ball; roll in nut mixture. Serve with crackers.

Makes 12 servings.

Brenda Ramsey

∎ *Sausage Strata* ∎

This is a tasty appetizer when cut into bite-size squares. I serve Sausage Strata along with a hot fruit compote, cheese grits and fresh baked blueberry muffins for brunch at our home. Friends always enjoy the food, and the hostess likes it because most items are made the night before!

6 slices bread
1 pound hot bulk pork sausage
1 teaspoon prepared mustard
1 cup (¼ pound) shredded mild cheese
3 eggs, beaten
1¼ cups milk
¾ cup half-and-half
½ teaspoon Worcestershire sauce
Dash each pepper, nutmeg and salt

Trim bread and place in bottom of greased 13x9x2-inch casserole. Brown and crumble sausage; drain. Stir in mustard. Spoon over bread; sprinkle with cheese. One and a half hours before cooking, combine eggs, milk, half-and-half, Worcestershire sauce, pepper, nutmeg and salt. Pour over cheese. Preheat oven to 350°. Bake for 30 to 35 minutes until set.

Makes 6 to 8 servings.

Florence McKeithan

Small towns like Lynchburg still enjoy street dances. The town square is roped off and people of all ages come to dance with friends and relatives. Everyone swings to the beat of the music. Those who don't dance just enjoy watching and being a part of this celebration.

▪ *Cocktail Meatballs* ▪

2 pounds ground beef
2 cups soft bread crumbs
2 eggs, beaten
½ onion, chopped
1 tablespoon parsley
2 teaspoons salt
  Margarine or butter
1 10-ounce jar apricot preserves
½ cup favorite barbecue sauce

Combine first 6 ingredients; mix thoroughly. Shape into 1-inch meatballs. Brown in a skillet with a little margarine to keep meatballs from sticking. Drain on paper towels. Place into a crockpot or chafing dish to keep hot. Combine preserves and barbecue sauce; pour over meatballs. Keep heat low, but high enough to keep hot for serving.
   Makes 10 to 12 servings.

Bonnie Darnell

▪ *Cheese-Sausage Balls* ▪

1 pound sharp cheese, grated and
  at room temperature
1 pound bulk sausage, mild or hot
3 cups biscuit mix

Preheat oven to 350°. Using a fork, mix cheese, sausage and biscuit mix. Shape into 1-inch balls and place on ungreased baking sheet. Bake for 12 to 15 minutes. Serve hot or cold.
   Makes 3 to 4 dozen.

Blanche Watson

23

▪ *Mock Crab Dip* ▪

1 large onion, finely chopped
1 cup mayonnaise
½ cup grated Parmesan cheese
Party rye bread slices

Combine first 3 ingredients and mix well. Toast one side of rye bread and then spread mixture on other side. Place under broiler until bubbly. Serve at once—delicious! Makes 2 dozen.

▪ *Hot Artichoke Dip* ▪

This is very easy, very unusual and will bring the hostess many compliments!

1 15-ounce can artichoke hearts
1 cup mayonnaise
1 cup grated Parmesan cheese
Garlic salt to taste
Crackers

Preheat oven to 350°. Drain artichoke hearts and chop into fine pieces. Add mayonnaise, cheese and garlic salt. Blend well. Pour into glass baking dish (round or oblong). Bake for about 20 minutes. Serve with wheat crackers, sesame seed crackers or other favorites. Makes 6 to 8 servings.

Wilma Bedford

▪ *Hot Crab, Artichoke and Jalapeño Dip With Pita Triangles* ▪

1 large green pepper, chopped
1 tablespoon vegetable oil
2 14-ounce cans artichoke hearts, drained and finely chopped
2 cups mayonnaise
½ cup thinly sliced scallions
½ cup drained and chopped pimiento
1 cup freshly grated Parmesan cheese
1½ tablespoons lemon juice (or to taste)
4 teaspoons Worcestershire sauce
3 pickled jalapeño peppers, drained, seeded and minced (use rubber gloves)
1 teaspoon celery salt
1 pound crabmeat, thawed, drained and cartilage picked out
⅓ cup sliced almonds
Pita triangles, toasted

In a small heavy skillet, cook pepper in oil over moderate heat, stirring until softened. Let cool. In a large bowl, combine the pepper, artichokes, mayonnaise, scallions, pimiento, Parmesan cheese, lemon juice, Worcestershire sauce, jalapeño peppers and celery salt. Blend mixture until well combined; gently stir in the crabmeat. Transfer mixture to a buttered ovenproof chafing dish or baking pan. Sprinkle with almonds. The dip may be prepared up to this point 1 day in advance and kept covered and chilled. When ready to serve, preheat oven to 375°. Bake for 25 to 30 minutes or until top is golden and mixture is bubbly. Serve with pita triangles. Makes 2 to 3 dozen.

Fran Houser

National Walking Horse Celebration

Margaret and Lynne Tolley

In the early days of Tennessee there were many distilleries dotting the hills and hollows where good water was available. One of these early distillers was named Tolley. Mr. Tolley still has many relatives in the area, and there's even a community in Lynchburg called Tolleytown. In a beautiful old home in the middle of Tolleytown live Margaret Tolley and her daughter Lynne. Visitors to the Jack Daniel Distillery remember Margaret as the hostess at the Welcome Center for many years. Now visitors to Lynchburg meet Margaret when they eat at Miss Mary Bobo's Boarding House, where Lynne is the proprietress and her mother is a hostess.

Food and hospitality have been of major importance in their lives. While growing up, Lynne was exposed to wonderful food prepared by her mother. Guests were plentiful in their home, and holidays called for bountiful dinners with extended family members coming many miles to celebrate. Today Lynne is a famous Tennessee hostess and preparation of wonderful food is a continued tradition at the Boarding House.

A favorite celebration for Lynne and Margaret is the ten-day National Walking Horse Celebration held in nearby Shelbyville each fall. For years they have had a reserved box, and they entertain friends and family each night during the celebration. Many Southern foods are sold at the concession stands. A favorite is country ham sandwiches, which they purchase each evening as a part of their festival tradition. However, a basket of finger foods is also prepared and taken with them to accompany the sandwiches.

The food and fun shared on these evenings, along with the beauty and splendor of the festival and the naming of a grand champion make this annual celebration their traditional favorite.

• *Tex-Mex Layer Dip* •

I'm always asked to bring this to our Christmas Eve family cocktail buffet—even after the hostess snubbed it the first year and placed it in the kitchen instead of on the dining room table. Men love it too!

1 cup sour cream
½ cup mayonnaise
1 package taco seasoning mix
3 medium avocados, diced
2 tablespoons lemon juice
  Salt and pepper to taste
2 cans plain jalapeño bean dip
1 large bunch chopped green
  onions
3 medium tomatoes, chopped
2 cans pitted, chopped ripe olives
1 8-ounce package sharp cheddar
  cheese (grated)
  Corn chips

Blend sour cream, mayonnaise and taco seasoning mix; set aside. Combine avocados, lemon juice, salt and pepper. Layer in order: bean dip, avocado mixture, sour cream mixture, onions, tomatoes, olives and cheese. Serve with corn chips!
  Makes 8 to 10 servings.

Sue Upchurch

• *Cheese Ball* •

2 1-pound boxes Velveeta cheese
2 8-ounce packages cream cheese
2 5-ounce jars Kraft Old English
  Sharp cheese
  Chopped onion, optional
  Chopped pecans

Combine cheeses in large bowl; set aside until room temperature. Mix cheeses thoroughly. Add some finely chopped onion, if desired. Shape into balls. Roll in chopped pecans. Wrap each ball in plastic wrap; place in small bowls and chill.
  Makes 2 cheese balls.

Judy Heslar

• *Ham and Cheese Ball* •

1 8-ounce package cream cheese
1 tablespoon salad dressing
  Worcestershire sauce and garlic
  powder to taste
1 cup grated cheddar cheese
½ cup grated Velveeta cheese
4 ounces chopped ham
1 bunch green onions, chopped
  part-way up the stem
  Finely chopped parsley

Mix cream cheese, salad dressing, Worcestershire sauce and garlic powder until creamy. Add next 4 ingredients. Form into a ball; roll in parsley.
  Makes 10 to 12 servings.

Debbie Strickland

▪ *Layered Tostada Dip* ▪

1 16-ounce can refried beans
½ teaspoon chili powder
2 avocados, peeled and mashed
½ cup Miracle Whip salad dressing
4 bacon slices, cooked crisp and
   crumbled
¼ cup chopped onion
½ teaspoon salt
   Dash hot pepper sauce
1 cup chopped ripe olives
1 cup chopped tomatoes
1 4-ounce can chopped green
   chilies
1 cup (4 ounces) shredded natural
   Monterey jack cheese
   Tortilla chips

Combine beans and chili powder; mix well and set aside. Combine avocados, salad dressing, bacon, onion and seasonings; mix well. Layer bean mixture, avocado mixture, olives, tomatoes, chilies and cheese in shallow bowl. Serve with tortilla chips.
   Makes 8 servings.

▪ *Beer Cheese* ▪

3 pounds American cheese
4 heaping tablespoons mayonnaise
18 ounces beer, at room
   temperature
1½ tablespoons chili powder
1½ tablespoons garlic
1 teaspoon cayenne pepper
2 tablespoons hot pepper sauce

Grind cheese in blender or food processor. Add mayonnaise and enough beer to make cheese begin to blend. Add remaining ingredients. Keep adding beer very slowly until desired consistency. Serve spread with assorted crackers or as a dip with vegetables.
   Makes 12 to 15 servings.

Kathy Woodard

▪ *Baked Crab and Shrimp* ▪

1 medium chopped green pepper
1 cup chopped celery
1 4½-ounce can shrimp, rinsed
   and drained
1 teaspoon Worcestershire sauce
⅛ teaspoon pepper
1 onion, chopped
1 6½-ounce can crab meat, drained
   and cartilage removed
1 cup mayonnaise
½ teaspoon salt
½ cup dry bread crumbs
1 teaspoon butter, melted

Preheat oven to 350°. Mix all ingredients, except bread crumbs and butter. Pour mixture into ungreased 1-quart casserole dish or six individual baking shells. Toss bread crumbs in melted butter; sprinkle over seafood mixture. Bake, uncovered, for 30 minutes.
   Makes 6 servings.

27

▪ SOUPS AND SALADS ▪

Soups and salads are some of the favorite dishes at celebrations. Look at the bounty of salads at a family reunion and you will realize how popular these are with one and all. Or consider that it is soup that is prepared most often to be taken to a sick friend or loved one. Just think how much better you feel when hot homemade soup prepared by loving hands is placed before you.

Soups and salads are considered in the culinary world to be "course dishes." However, this distinction hasn't caught on with the population at large. Soup, when served at home, is the main dish and nothing but hot bread and a drink is needed to round out a meal. Salads also can be main dishes as with "Hot Chicken Salad."

Memorable dishes can be as fun as a "Mexican Pyramid," which is a fun party salad, or as simple as "Mom's Potato Soup," which can bring to mind very special nights when the family mood was one of belonging. Either way, the soups and salads here have given many families warm, satisfying memories of foods that were nourishing to both the body and the spirit.

▪ *Mystery Soup* ▪

2 13½-ounce cans beef broth
1 8-ounce package cream cheese,
  softened

Combine ingredients in saucepan. Heat; mix well. Serve hot or cold—excellent.
Makes 4 servings.

▪ *Maryland Crab Soup* ▪

¾ cup diced carrots
½ cup diced celery
¾ cup diced onions
1 cup diced cabbage
2½ cups diced red and green
  peppers
½ cup olive oil
2 tablespoons tomato paste
2 28-ounce cans plum tomatoes,
  drained and chopped
2 quarts plus 6 ounces fish stock
  or clam juice
2 teaspoons fennel seed
2 teaspoons thyme
12 ounces frozen peas
1 pound crabmeat (backfin), picked
  clean of shell
1 teaspoon cayenne pepper
1 tablespoon Old Bay seasoning

Sauté carrots, celery, onion, cabbage and peppers in olive oil until tender. Add tomato paste and chopped tomatoes. Cook for 3 to 4 minutes. Add stock, fennel seed and thyme; simmer soup for about 45 minutes. Remove from heat; add peas and crabmeat. Stir in cayenne and Old Bay seasoning. Adjust seasonings to taste.
Makes 1 gallon.

Karen Moran

▪ *Mom's Potato Soup* ▪

Childhood memories of cold winters with wind gusting outside, a blazing fire inside and my mother, sister and brother eating Mom's wonderful homemade soup—a special treat just for us when Daddy worked late into the evening—still makes soup a special treat.

6 medium russet or Idaho potatoes
1 large onion, chopped
2 stalks celery with tops, cut into
  ½-inch pieces
  Salt and fresh cracked pepper to
  taste
1 stick butter
2 cups heavy cream
  Saltines

Peel potatoes and cut into chunks; cover with water in a 3- to 4-quart soup or saucepan. Add onion, celery, salt, and pepper. Boil until potatoes are just done (water should be reduced and some of the smaller pieces of potato will be breaking down to thicken the soup). Add butter in pieces for easier melting; lower heat to medium and add cream. Heat through, but do not boil. Ladle into soup bowls and serve with pepper and saltines.
Makes 4 to 6 servings.

30

• *Salmon Soup* •

2½ cups half-and-half
2 tablespoons butter
1 6.5-ounce can red sockeye
  salmon, drained
  Salt and fresh cracked pepper to
  taste
  Saltines

Place half-and-half in saucepan to heat slowly (be careful not to boil). Add butter and salmon. Try to keep the salmon in two large chunks. Heat just until hot. Remove salmon with spatula into two bowls; divide soup evenly between the two bowls. Serve with salt, pepper and saltines.
Makes 2 servings.

Hope Powell

• *Cheddar Soup with Ham and Jalapeños* •

1 cup diced carrots
1 cup diced celery
3 to 4 diced jalapeños
1 stick butter
¼ cup all-purpose flour
2 quarts chicken stock
1 pound grated cheddar cheese
1 cup heavy cream
1 tablespoon Worcestershire sauce
1 tablespoon dry mustard
½ cup dark beer
1½ ounces grated Parmesan cheese
½ pound diced ham
1 cup diced scallions
  Salt to taste
  Hot pepper sauce to taste

Sauté carrots, celery and jalapeños in butter until tender. Add flour slowly to the vegetables; whisk frequently for about 6 minutes. Add stock; slowly whisking while pouring. Simmer for about 25 minutes. Remove soup from heat and whisk in cheese, a small amount at a time until mixture is smooth. Blend in cream. Add Worcestershire sauce, mustard, beer and Parmesan cheese. Whisk until well blended. Add ham and scallions. Season with salt and hot sauce. *Note:* For a thinner soup, add more stock if desired.
Makes 1 gallon.

Jayne Young

• *Cabbage Soup* •

1 pound lean ground beef
1 medium onion, chopped
2 cloves garlic, crushed
1 14½-ounce can tomatoes
1 15-ounce can tomato sauce
1 16-ounce can kidney beans
1 tablespoon parsley
½ teaspoon sweet basil
1½ tablespoons chili powder
  Salt and pepper to taste
1 medium head cabbage, shredded

Brown ground beef with onion and garlic; drain off excess fat. Place tomatoes in blender; chop coarsely. Add tomatoes and remaining ingredients to beef. Simmer for 1 hour, or in slow cooker for 2½ hours on low.
Makes 8 servings.

Diane Dickey

31

■ *Beef Borscht* ■

2 pounds beef (preferably chuck or
  brisket) cut into ½-inch cubes
  Salt to taste
  Black pepper to taste
½ cup olive oil
2 pounds diced cabbage
2 cups diced onions
2 tablespoons minced garlic
⅔ cup red wine vinegar
3 quarts veal stock
2 28-ounce cans canned tomatoes,
  drained, chopped and liquid
  reserved
½ cup packed brown sugar
1½ tablespoons finely chopped fresh
  thyme
2 bay leaves
2 16-ounce cans shoestring beets,
  drained and liquid reserved
⅓ cup lemon juice or to taste

Lightly season cut beef with salt and pepper. In a Dutch oven or heavy soup pot, heat olive oil until just smoking. Sear meat on all sides to brown evenly. Add cabbage, onion and garlic; sauté with meat just until tender. Add red wine vinegar, veal stock, tomatoes, brown sugar, thyme and bay leaves. Simmer for 1 hour to 1 hour and 15 minutes or until meat is tender. Add beets and season with lemon juice, salt and pepper. The juice from the beets and tomatoes can be added at end of cooking time, if you prefer more of a broth-like soup.

Makes 1 gallon.

Patricia Tolley

■ *Fresh Spinach Salad* ■

1 cup vegetable oil
5 tablespoons red wine vinegar
4 tablespoons sour cream
2 cloves garlic, crushed
½ teaspoon dry mustard
1½ teaspoons salt
2 tablespoons sugar
  Fresh cracked pepper
2 teaspoons chopped parsley
1 bunch fresh spinach, stemmed,
  washed and drained
6 slices bacon, cooked crisp and
  crumbled
1 small red onion, sliced into rings
2 tomatoes, peeled and sliced
10 fresh mushrooms, sliced
3 eggs, hard-boiled and finely
  chopped

Combine first 9 ingredients; mix well. Just before serving, combine spinach, bacon and onion rings; toss lightly to mix. Pour dressing, reserving small amount, over salad and toss again. Top salad with tomato slices, mushrooms and eggs. Pour reserved dressing over and serve.

Makes 8 servings.

▪ *Wilted Lettuce* ▪

2 cups torn leaf lettuce
2 cups Boston or bibb lettuce
3 small green onions, chopped
5 slices bacon
2 tablespoons vinegar
1½ teaspoons sugar

Combine lettuces which have been torn into small bite-size pieces. Toss with green onions. Fry bacon until crisp; drain on paper towels. Crumble into a small bowl. Reserve bacon drippings. Add vinegar and sugar to bacon drippings in pan; heat to boiling. Pour hot dressing over lettuce; top with crumbled bacon and serve immediately.
Makes 6 servings.

▪ *Hot Chicken Salad* ▪

8 cups diced, cooked chicken
2 teaspoons salt
2 cups diced celery
1½ cups chopped green pepper, optional
1½ cups chopped almonds
2 cups mayonnaise
2 10½-ounce cans cream of chicken soup
4 hard-boiled eggs, chopped
1½ cups crushed potato chips
1 cup grated sharp cheese

Preheat oven to 350°. Mix chicken, salt, celery, green pepper, almonds, mayonnaise, soup and eggs. Place in large casserole dish; top with potato chips and cheese. Bake for 25 minutes. This is good served in baked pastry shells.
Makes 20 servings.

Mary Stanfill

▪ *Catfish Salad* ▪

2 farm-raised catfish fillets, cut into 1-inch cubes
1 yellow or red pepper, roasted and cut into strips
1 small red onion, sliced into rings
1 tablespoon chopped fresh dill (or 1½ teaspoons dried)
¼ cup olive oil
¼ cup balsamic or red wine vinegar
1 head Boston lettuce, torn
2 cups arugula or romaine leaves torn
4 strips lean bacon, cooked crisp and crumbled
3 ounces bleu cheese, crumbled
Salt and pepper

Place catfish cubes in skillet; add water to cover. Simmer for 5 to 7 minutes or until catfish flakes easily with a fork. Drain. In a large bowl, combine catfish cubes, pepper strips, onion rings, dill, oil and vinegar. Cover; marinate for 1 hour. Just before serving, toss with lettuce leaves, arugula, bacon and bleu cheese. Salt and pepper to taste.
Makes 4 servings.

Omenia Copeland

33

▪ *Slaw* ▪

1 cup vinegar
⅔ cup vegetable oil
1 tablespoon salt
1 teaspoon dry mustard
1 teaspoon sugar
1 teaspoon mustard seed
1 large head cabbage, shredded

Heat vinegar, oil, salt, mustard, sugar and mustard seed. Pour over shredded cabbage. Chill. This slaw will keep in the refrigerator a long time. It is especially good with barbecue.
Makes 6 to 8 servings.

Jane Osborne

▪ *Bess' Cole Slaw* ▪

1 large head cabbage, shredded
  fine
1 medium onion, cut in bite-size
  pieces
¾ cup sugar
1 cup vinegar
1 tablespoon mustard seed
1 tablespoon celery seed
1 tablespoon sugar
1½ tablespoons salt
1 cup vegetable oil

Combine cabbage and onion; sprinkle sugar on top. Set aside. Bring remaining ingredients, except oil, to a boil. Add oil. Bring again to a boil. Pour over cabbage while hot. Cover tightly. This will keep several days in refrigerator.
Makes 6 to 8 servings.

Mabel Jones

▪ *Teddy's Favorite Salad* ▪

This is the perfect salad to accompany Moody Ranch Chicken *(page 61). With this salad, garlic bread and the chicken dish, you have a whole meal, perfect for a party menu.*

2 ripe tomatoes
1 green pepper
1 large cucumber
1 can artichoke hearts, drained
4 strips bacon, cooked crisp and
  crumbled
  Lawry's seasoned salt
  Black or cracked pepper
1 head iceberg lettuce
1 bunch green leaf lettuce
  Italian dressing
  Parmesan cheese

Chop tomatoes, pepper, cucumber and artichoke hearts. Add bacon to chopped vegetables. Season with Lawry's salt and pepper. Cover and place in refrigerator. Wash lettuce and pat dry. Mix vegetables with lettuce; top with Italian dressing and Parmesan cheese.
Makes 6 to 8 servings.

Teddy Heard Orr

34

Mr. Jack Daniel's Original Silver Cornet Band

For any occasion where the whole community comes together to celebrate, you can be sure that a band will be playing. It may be a football game, a school play, a circus, a fair, a street dance, or a parade. The band might be a professional one, the high school marching band, or the hometown band made up of amateur players of all ages. At the turn of the century Lynchburg had just such a band—one made up of players representing almost every business in town. Today's band is a recreation of the band that was actually begun by Mr. Jack Daniel back in 1892.

Mr. Jack Daniel's Original Silver Cornet Band has played at hometown celebrations all across America and has done a grand job. It has played at a Fourth of July celebration at the White House and at the Festival of Lights in honor of Thomas A. Edison in Fort Myers, Florida. The band members have tootled and flourished on such occasions as Disneyland's American Music Festival, the Sacramento International Dixieland Jubilee, the French Quarter Festival in New Orleans, Chautauqua's SummerFest, Chicago's State Street Festival, Newport's Summer Classical Festival, and the Great American Brass Band Festival.

Whatever show they bring to the stage — Hometown Saturday Night, Hometown Christmas, Hometown Homecoming, or Hometown Almanac — it promises to be fun. This sterling ensemble of artists with a crusty old professor leading them takes their hometown of Lynchburg to hometowns in every state. One thing is sure. Feet tap and hands clap when the band begins to play and everyone has a grand time, including the band!

▪ *Salade Bonne Femme* ▪

1 cup diced Swiss cheese
4 large potatoes, boiled, peeled and
  cubed
½ cup chopped celery, including
  tops of stalks
¼ cup chopped nuts
½ cup mayonnaise
1 tablespoon prepared mustard
1 teaspoon Worcestershire sauce

Combine first four ingredients in salad bowl. Combine remaining ingredients; blend well. Pour over potato mixture. Chill until serving time.
  Makes 6 to 8 servings.

Wildred Patton

▪ *Summer Salad* ▪

2 medium apples, peeled, cored
  and diced
1 small onion, diced
1 green pepper, diced
1 5-ounce can chicken or turkey
3 cups cooked macaroni, well
  drained
  Mayonnaise or salad dressing

Mix all ingredients together thoroughly using enough mayonnaise to moisten. Serve with crackers, if desired. *Note:* Since this is a cold salad, it can be made hours in advance and leftovers are just as good the next day!
  Makes 6 to 8 servings.

Brenda Ramsey

▪ *Corn Salad* ▪

2 11-ounce cans white whole
  kernel or shoe-peg corn, well
  drained
1 bunch green onions, chopped
  (green tops, too!)
½ to ¾ cup mayonnaise (not salad
  dressing)

Mix all ingredients well; chill. *Note:* Recipe can be halved, doubled, etc., to feed everybody. It keeps well in the refrigerator for several days.
  Makes 4 to 6 servings.

Kathy Woodard

▪ *Buttermilk Salad* ▪

1 6-ounce box strawberry-flavor
  gelatin
2 cups buttermilk
1 20-ounce can crushed pineapple
1 cup chopped pecans
1 9-ounce container Cool Whip

In large saucepan, mix gelatin, buttermilk and pineapple. Heat until dissolved (do not boil). Set aside and cool; add nuts and Cool Whip. Blend, but do not beat. Pour into a 13x9x2-inch dish and chill. *Note:* Other flavors of gelatin may be used, if desired.
  Makes 8 servings.

Marsha Russell

▪ *Congealed Asparagus Salad* ▪

This is an unusual salad recipe that my family enjoys.

1 cup water
1 cup sugar
½ cup white vinegar
½ teaspoon salt
3 envelopes plain gelatin
¾ cup cold water
1 cup finely chopped celery
½ cup chopped nuts
1 2-ounce jar pimiento, drained
   and chopped
1 tablespoon grated onion
1 15½-ounce can cut asparagus

Bring first 4 ingredients to a rolling boil in saucepan. Mix gelatin with ¾ cup cold water. Add to ingredients in saucepan, stirring to blend. Chill until it is a soft jelly-like consistency. Add celery, nuts, pimiento and onion; stir to mix. Add asparagus; toss salad lightly with a fork. Pour into an oiled mold or serving dish; chill until serving time.
   Makes 6 to 8 servings.

Mary Trice

▪ *Peaches 'N' Cream Salad* ▪

2 3-ounce boxes lemon-flavor
   gelatin, divided
2 cups boiling water, divided
1 3-ounce package cream cheese
1 cup heavy cream
2 tablespoons sugar
1 cup orange juice
½ cup chopped pecans
1 1-pound 6-ounce can peach pie
   filling

Dissolve 1 package lemon gelatin in 1 cup boiling water. Pour into bowl with cream cheese. Beat with mixer. Whip cream; sweeten with 2 tablespoons sugar. Add orange juice and whipped cream to cream cheese mixture; beat with mixer. Stir in pecans. Pour into 13x9x2-inch pan or mold. Chill until firm. Dissolve second box of gelatin in 1 cup boiling water. Add pie filling; cool. Pour over first layer; chill until firm.
   Makes 12 servings.

Elizabeth Bonner

▪ *Confederate Mousse* ▪

5 large cucumbers
2 cups ginger ale, divided
1 6-ounce box lime-flavor gelatin
2 envelopes plain gelatin
1 tablespoon sugar
1 cup sour cream
1 cup mayonnaise
   Hot pepper sauce
   Lettuce leaves
   Tomatoes

Peel and chop cucumbers; drain for 1 hour. Add 1 cup ginger ale. Heat remaining ginger ale; dissolve gelatins in hot ginger ale. Add to cucumber mixture; cool. Mix next 4 ingredients using a good splash of the hot pepper sauce. Pour into a large loaf mold; chill. To serve, unmold onto platter lined with lettuce leaves. Garnish with sliced fresh tomatoes.
   Makes 12 servings.

Picnics are pure summertime pleasure. Friends and family gather in the backyard or in the local park. Food can be from a hamper and as simple as sandwiches and chips, or mom just might bring the pot roast and all the trimmings outside for dinner. Whatever the food, picnics are an occasion that celebrates a simple and less complicated time. They are food for our soul.

▪ *Tomato Shrimp Mold* ▪

1 10¾-ounce can condensed tomato soup
1 8-ounce package cream cheese
1 3-ounce package cream cheese
2 tablespoons plain gelatin
2 cans shrimp, drained and juice reserved
1 cup mayonnaise
1 cup chopped celery
1 cup chopped green pepper
1 cup chopped onion
Olives
Crackers

Heat soup and cream cheese slowly. Beat with hand mixer for 1 minute. Soak gelatin in shrimp juice and enough water to make ½ cup liquid. Pour gelatin into soup mixture. Add mayonnaise, shrimp, celery, pepper and onion. Pour into lightly greased fish-shaped mold; cover with plastic wrap and chill overnight. Unmold carefully onto a large tray and garnish with olive halves for eyes. Serve with crackers.

Makes 12 servings.

Marian Baird

▪ *Frozen Waldorf Salad* ▪

Waldorf Salad is our family favorite. This is a new rendition of an old classic.

1 8-ounce can crushed pineapple
2 eggs, beaten
½ cup sugar
⅛ teaspoon salt
2 large apples, peeled, cored and cubed
¼ cup lemon juice
1 cup chopped celery
½ cup broken walnuts
1 cup heavy cream, whipped
Lettuce leaves

Drain pineapple and reserve juice. Add enough water to juice to make ½ cup. Combine juice, beaten eggs, sugar and salt in saucepan. Stirring constantly, cook over medium heat until thickened. Cool. Toss apples in lemon juice. Add pineapple, celery, apples and walnuts to cooled mixture; stir to mix well. Fold into whipped cream. Spoon into an 8-inch square dish; cover and freeze. To serve, remove from freezer and let stand at room temperature for 30 minutes. Cut into squares and serve on lettuce leaves.

Makes 9 servings.

▪ *Aunt Lucille's Strawberry Salad* ▪

Aunt Lucille is my Daddy's sister. She has always been a woman of great heart and pride. Her heart has led her to have many friends, whom she entertains with great hospitality. Her pride is always visible in the beauty of her table and the wonderful food that she prepares.

2 3-ounce boxes strawberry-flavor
  gelatin, divided
1 15-ounce can crushed pineapple,
  drained
1 banana, mashed
½ cup chopped pecans
1 8-ounce package frozen
  strawberries
2 cups sour cream
  Lettuce leaves

Prepare one package of gelatin and pour into a flat dish. Place in refrigerator to set until firm. Prepare remaining gelatin and place in refrigerator; jell to consistency of egg white. Beat this mixture with egg beater; fold in pineapple, banana, nuts and strawberries. Spread sour cream over plain gelatin, then top with fruit-mixed gelatin. Chill until firm. Cut into squares; serve on lettuce leaves.
  Makes 8 servings.

Lucille Phelps

▪ *Orange Sherbet Salad* ▪

2 3-ounce packages pineapple-
  orange-flavor gelatin
2 cups boiling water
1 11-ounce can mandarin orange
  sections, drained and juice
  reserved
1 envelope unflavored gelatin
1 pint orange sherbet
  Pinch of salt

Dissolve pineapple-orange gelatin in boiling water along with the juice from the orange sections. Soften unflavored gelatin in cold water, according to directions; add to hot gelatin mixture. Beat in orange sherbet until well dissolved. Add salt and oranges. Pour into greased 6-cup mold. Chill.
  Makes 8 servings.

Blanche Watson

▪ *Dreamy Apricot Salad* ▪

2 3-ounce boxes apricot-flavor
  gelatin
⅔ cup sugar
⅔ cup water
2 4¾-ounce jars apricot baby food
1 20-ounce can crushed pineapple,
  undrained
1 14-ounce can sweetened
  condensed milk
1 8-ounce package cream cheese,
  softened
1 cup chopped nuts

Combine gelatin, sugar and water in saucepan. Bring to a boil, stirring to dissolve. Remove from heat; stir in baby food and crushed pineapple. Place in refrigerator to cool. Combine milk and cream cheese; beat until smooth. Stir in cooled gelatin mixture, then nuts. Pour into a 9-cup mold; chill until firm.
  Makes 20 servings.

Marte Sanders

39

▪ *Easy Fruit Salad* ▪

Easy, quick and delicious are good ways to describe this fruit salad. A family favorite for many years this salad is ideal for mealtime, picnics, potluck suppers and even as a topping for ice cream.

1 21-ounce can peach pie filling
1 15¼-ounce can pineapple chunks, drained
2 6¼-ounce cans mandarin oranges, drained
1 teaspoon lemon juice
½ cup sugar
4 or 5 medium bananas, sliced
½ cup raisins, optional
Maraschino cherries

Combine pie filling, pineapple and oranges. Combine lemon juice and sugar. Pour over bananas. Mix with fruits. Garnish with maraschino cherries. This is best if prepared at least 4 or 5 hours prior to serving.
Makes 8 servings.

Delene Stone

▪ *Marte's Cranberry Salad* ▪

1 pound fresh cranberries
1 large seedless orange
1 cup sugar
½ cup chopped walnuts
½ cup chopped celery
3 cups water, divided
1 6-ounce box plus 1 3-ounce box red raspberry-flavor gelatin

Chop cranberries and orange; mix in sugar, nuts and celery. In small saucepan, bring 1½ cups water to boil. Stir in gelatin; remove from heat and stir until dissolved. Stir in remaining 1½ cups water. Add to cranberry mixture. Pour into mold and chill until firm.
Makes 6 to 8 servings.

Marthella Sanders

▪ *Cranberry Ambrosia* ▪

This dish is especially good with turkey and dressing and the traditional Thanksgiving Dinner.

1 package cranberries, ground
2 cups sugar
1 cup chopped nuts
1 cup chopped seedless grapes
1 pint heavy cream, whipped

Mix cranberries and sugar well; let stand overnight. Drain for 1 hour. Add remaining ingredients. Mix well and serve.
Makes 6 to 8 servings.

Mary Ruth Hall

40

▪ *Tuna Fish Salad Mold* ▪

1 package lemon-flavored gelatin
2 cups hot water
2 tablespoons vinegar
½ teaspoon salt
1 cup tuna fish, flaked
1 cup celery, chopped
2 tablespoons pimiento, chopped
½ cup chopped nuts
½ cup mayonnaise
  Lettuce leaves

Dissolve gelatin in hot water. Add vinegar and salt. Chill. When slightly thickened, add remaining ingredients, except lettuce. Mix well. Turn into a 1-quart mold or 8 individual molds. Chill. Unmold. Serve on lettuce leaves.

Makes 8 servings.

Ilene Brown

▪ *Mexican Pyramids* ▪

Here is a party dish if ever there was one. Just have the ingredients ready and line them up as stated. Everyone takes a plate and makes their own salad. The ingredients are different, but they make this salad special, so have a little south-of-the-border fun. I serve this at bridge luncheons or Sunday school class parties. It is a good conversation starter.

4 pounds lean ground chuck
3 medium onions, chopped
2 16-ounce cans tomatoes
1 12-ounce can tomato paste
2 tablespoons garlic salt
1 20-ounce can Mexican-style
  ranch beans

Brown meat and onion together in skillet. Add next 4 ingredients and simmer for 1 hour over low heat. For party, line up the following dishes in the order given. Give everyone a plate and let them make the pyramids.

Pyramid order:
Large package of small Fritos, (not dip-size)
3 cups cooked rice
Meat and beans as prepared above
1½ pounds cheddar cheese, grated
2 heads lettuce, shredded
5 tomatoes, peeled and chopped
3 onions, chopped
2 10-ounce jars stuffed olives
1½ cups chopped pecans
1 16-ounce package shredded coconut
2 8-ounce jars picante sauce

Makes 10 to 12 servings.

41

• BREADS •

Homebaked bread is more nostalgic than any other food. It awakens all of our senses. Pillsbury's advertising slogan "Nothin' says lovin' like somethin' from the oven" is true. Every bread recipe we received for this book had with it a note on memories of love, comfort, security, and warmth. However, with the exception of quick breads like muffins or biscuits, few cooks are still carrying on the homemade bread tradition. We found that most of the bread recipes were generally referred to as memorable (past) favorites, as in "my grandmother's bread" or "my mama made. . . ."

Trying all of these recipes, we found that families today are like those of past generations. Our kitchen became a gathering place when we started baking bread. Great interest was generated by fragrant smells from the oven and a favorite pastime was peering into the oven's glass window and uttering sounds like *oooh* and *aaah* to express ecstacy. Butter disappeared faster than cold drinks, and "testing the recipe" beat chips and dips by a country mile.

But more than this, we received great satisfaction from producing a browned-to-perfection loaf, a beautiful golden braid, or a pan of fresh fragrant rolls. Besides this satisfaction, a cook will find making yeast bread to be a great stress reliever. You can really get into the kneading. It is an activity worth rediscovering because nothing spells "special occasion" like homebaked bread.

When election time comes to Lynchburg, anyone who wants to watch can take part in the celebration. County clerk . . . governor . . . the names of all those running for office are posted on a blackboard outside the courthouse. The whole town turns out to watch the results as the election districts count the votes.

■ *Lawn Party Loaf Bread* ■

Lawn parties were favorite summer occasions when my grandmother was a girl. Little sandwiches, fruit salad or melon slices, and desserts were the traditional fare. This was her favorite bread recipe for these sandwiches.

When we were little, she would make pineapple cream cheese filling by mixing eight ounces of cream cheese and one small can of crushed pineapple, using enough juice to make it smooth and light. This made our little tea parties an absolute delight.

1 cup scalded milk
1 package dry yeast
¾ cup sugar, divided
6 cups all-purpose flour
½ teaspoon salt
⅔ cup soft butter
1 egg, plus 1 additional yolk
1 teaspoon vanilla
1 egg yolk beaten with 1 teaspoon water

Scald milk in saucepan. Do not boil. Remove from heat; cool to lukewarm. Add yeast and 2 tablespoons sugar to ¼ cup of the warm milk; set aside for the yeast to activate and bubbles to form. Combine flour, remaining sugar, salt and butter in large bread bowl. Add yeast mixture, remaining milk, egg, egg yolk and vanilla. Beat with mixer or by hand until blisters appear on dough and it no longer sticks to side of bowl. Cover and set in a warm place to rise for about 20 to 30 minutes. Punch dough down; knead on floured board for 3 or 4 minutes. Place in a greased loaf pan and allow to rise again. Preheat oven to 400°. Brush top with beaten egg yolk mixture. Bake on middle oven rack for about 1 hour or until golden brown. Cool and slice.

Makes 1 loaf.

Doris Lynch

44

■ *Braided Bread Loaf* ■

1 package dry yeast
1 cup warm water (110°)
5 tablespoons sugar
½ cup solid shortening, melted
1 whole egg, plus 1 egg white
¾ teaspoon salt
3½ cups all purpose flour, divided

Dissolve yeast in warm water in a large mixing bowl. Add sugar, shortening, whole egg, salt and half the flour. Beat on low speed with electric mixer (or by hand with wooden spoon). Stir in enough remaining flour to make a soft dough. Place dough in a greased bowl, turning once to grease top. Cover and let rise in a warm place for 1 hour or until doubled in bulk. (Dough may be covered and refrigerated for up to 5 days at this point, before letting rise.) Punch dough down; turn out onto a lightly floured board. Knead dough four or five times. Divide dough into equal thirds. Shape each third into a rope about 12 inches long. Place ropes on a greased baking sheet, being careful not to stretch. Pinch ropes together at one end to seal. Braid ropes together; pinch ends to seal. Cover and let rise in a warm place for about 30 minutes or until doubled in bulk. Preheat oven to 350°. Combine egg white with 1 tablespoon water; beat until frothy. Gently brush egg mixture on loaf top. Bake for 25 to 30 minutes. When done, bread will sound hollow when tapped.

Makes 1 loaf.

Dorothy Overstreet

■ *Celebration Bread* ■

Celebration Bread is well named. This is a wonderful sweet bread and is a favorite of ours. Hot bread was almost a celebration in itself, but this bread was baked for special holidays or family get-togethers. Grandma used the hometown product to enhance the flavor . . . and aroma. Since Grandad worked at Jack Daniel's that made the flavor even better to us!

4 cups sifted all-purpose flour
2 teaspoons baking powder
1 teaspoon baking soda
1 teaspoon salt
1¼ cups sugar
⅔ cup solid shortening
3 eggs
2 cups applesauce
2 teaspoons Jack Daniel's Whiskey
1 cup chopped pecans
1 16-ounce can pitted cherries,
   well drained
1 cup confectioners' sugar
2 tablespoons Jack Daniel's
   Whiskey
1 tablespoon butter

Preheat oven to 350°. Combine flour, baking powder, soda and salt in large bowl. In large mixing bowl, beat sugar and shortening until smooth and creamy. Add eggs and beat well. Add flour mixture alternately with the applesauce and 2 teaspoons Jack Daniel's Whiskey. Stir in nuts and drained cherries. Pour batter into 2 greased 9x5x3-inch loaf pans. Bake for 45 to 60 minutes or until a skewer inserted in center comes out clean. Remove from pans while warm; cool on wire rack. Blend remaining ingredients until smooth; spread on loaves.

Makes 2 loaves.

Oat Bran-Wheat Bread

2 packages dry yeast
2½ cups warm water
2 egg whites
¼ cup vegetable oil
¼ cup packed brown sugar
¼ cup molasses
1 cup oat bran
3 cups wheat flour
2 cups all-purpose flour or more

Dissolve yeast in warm water. Add egg whites, oil, brown sugar, molasses, oat bran and half the wheat flour. Mix with electric mixer (easiest to use dough hook— but you can mix with regular beaters at this stage). Add rest of wheat flour and enough white flour to make a kneadable consistency using dough hook or wooden spoon (if too thick for regular beaters). Let dough rise until doubled in bulk. Punch down; divide dough in half. Knead each half. Shape into loaves; place in greased and floured loaf pans. Let rise to desired size. Preheat oven to 375°. Bake for 45 minutes. *Note:* 1 tablespoon salt may be added if desired.

Makes 2 loaves.

Julie Walsh

Carrot-Pineapple Bread

This is a very moist and delicious bread.

1½ cups all-purpose flour
1 cup sugar
1 teaspoon baking powder
1 teaspoon baking soda
1 teaspoon ground cinnamon
¼ teaspoon salt
2 eggs, beaten
1 cup vegetable oil
1 cup grated raw carrots
½ cup crushed pineapple, undrained
1 teaspoon vanilla

Preheat oven to 350°. Combine first 6 ingredients in a large mixing bowl; stir in remaining ingredients. Beat on medium speed with electric mixer for 2 minutes. Pour into a greased and floured 9x5x3-inch loaf pan. Bake for 50 to 55 minutes or until a skewer inserted in center comes out clean.

Makes 1 loaf.

Bobbie Payne

The Fourth of July can be described in four words: family, food, flags, and fireworks — which all add up to fun. And in Lynchburg it also means Frontier Days, an annual celebration with a big parade, fried chicken and potato salad, watermelon fresh from the field, and homemade ice cream. Kids young and old enjoy the day and fireworks are the perfect finale.

▪ *Lemon Bread* ▪

½ cup solid shortening
1⅓ cups sugar, divided
2 eggs, beaten
½ cup milk
1½ cups all-purpose flour
1 teaspoon baking powder
¼ teaspoon salt
2 tablespoons grated lemon peel,
   divided
Juice of 1 lemon

Preheat oven to 350°. Cream shortening and 1 cup sugar. Add eggs and milk; mix well. In a separate bowl, combine dry ingredients with 1 tablespoon lemon peel. Slowly stir dry ingredients into creamed mixture; mix well. Pour batter into a greased and floured loaf pan and bake for approximately 30 minutes or until a skewer inserted in center comes out clean. Combine lemon juice, 1 tablespoon peel and remaining ⅓ cup sugar to make glaze. Remove bread from pan while still hot and place on aluminum foil. Spoon glaze over hot loaf; immediately wrap in foil. Refrigerate loaf while hot and chill overnight before serving.
Makes 1 loaf.

Mary Edwards

▪ *Orange Rolls* ▪

1 package dry yeast
¼ cup very warm water
1 cup sugar, divided
1 teaspoon salt
2 eggs
½ cup sour cream
1 stick butter or margarine,
   divided
3½ cups sifted all-purpose flour
2 tablespoons grated orange peel
Glaze (recipe follows)

Dissolve yeast in very warm water in large mixing bowl. Beat in ¼ cup sugar, salt, eggs, sour cream and 6 tablespoons of butter. Gradually add 2 cups flour. Beat until smooth. Knead remaining flour into dough. Let rise in a greased bowl in warm place until smooth. Knead dough on floured surface about 15 times. Roll half the dough out to form a 12-inch circle. Combine remaining ¾ cup sugar and orange peel. Brush dough with 1 tablespoon melted butter; sprinkle with half the orange-sugar mixture. Cut into 12 wedges. Roll each wedge up, starting with the wide end. Repeat with remaining dough. Cover and let rise in warm place for about 1 hour. Preheat oven to 350°. Bake for 20 minutes or until golden brown. Top with glaze.
Makes 2 dozen.

Phyllis Grider

Glaze

1 cup confectioners' sugar
2 tablespoons light cream
1 tablespoon melted butter

Blend all ingredients well; spread on warm rolls.
Makes 2 dozen.

• *Sour Cream Coffee Cake* •

When the University of Texas Longhorns have a daytime sporting event on television, the Men's Athletic Department staff can be found congregating at Bebe and Jack Boone's house for brunch and watching the game. Their friends are treated to Jack and Bebe's world-class omelets and Sour Cream Coffee Cake. Whether the game is a victory or not, the brunch is a sure-fire winner every time.

1 stick butter
1 cup sugar
2 eggs
1 cup sour cream
2 teaspoons vanilla
1½ cups all-purpose flour
1 tablespoon baking powder
1 teaspoon baking soda
½ cup chopped pecans
½ cup sugar
2 teaspoons cinnamon

Preheat oven to 350°. Cream butter and sugar. Add eggs one at a time. Stir in sour cream and vanilla. Sift flour, baking powder and soda together. Add to sour cream mixture. Grease an 8x8-inch pan. Pour in half the batter. Combine next 3 ingredients. Sprinkle half the nut mixture on the batter in pan. Add remaining batter. Top with remaining nut mixture. Bake for about 40 minutes or until a skewer inserted in center comes out clean.
    Makes 12 servings.

Bebe Boone

• *Miss Berta's Pumpkin Bread* •

1 cup melted shortening
2 cups pumpkin
1 cup dates, optional
4 eggs, beaten
1 cup water
1 cup nuts
3 cups sugar
2 teaspoons baking soda
½ teaspoon baking powder
2 teaspoons cinnamon
1 teaspoon nutmeg
1 teaspoon ginger
½ teaspoon ground cloves
½ teaspoon salt
3½ cups all-purpose flour

Preheat oven to 350°. Combine all ingredients. Mix thoroughly. Pour into greased loaf pans. Bake for 25 to 30 minutes or until a skewer inserted in center comes out clean.
    Makes 2 loaves.

Berta Costello

■ *Strawberry Bread* ■

3 cups all-purpose flour
2 cups sugar
½ teaspoon salt
1 teaspoon baking soda
1 tablespoon cinnamon
4 eggs, beaten
1¼ cups vegetable oil
1 16-ounce package frozen
   strawberries, thawed and drained
   (reserve 1 tablespoon syrup for
   glaze)
½ cup chopped pecans
1 cup confectioners' sugar
2 tablespoons lemon juice

Preheat oven to 350°. Sift together flour, sugar, salt, soda and cinnamon; set aside. Combine eggs and oil; mix well. Add sifted dry ingredients and mix well. Add strawberries and pecans; blend just until mixed. Pour into two 9x5-inch (or five 3x5-inch) greased and floured loaf pans. Bake for 45 to 50 minutes (20 minutes for mini-loaf pans). Bread is done when skewer inserted in center comes out clean. Do not overbake. Make glaze by combining confectioners' sugar, lemon juice and reserved strawberry syrup. Mix until smooth. Pour glaze over warm loaves; turn out of pan when cool.
   Makes 2 loaves.

Mona Hendley

■ *Church Breakfast Scones* ■

The name of this recipe tells you exactly what makes it special. For years, the men of our church have had prayer breakfasts. The only women who attend these are the ones who come to prepare the food. I started making these scones a long time ago for those occasions. I don't know if it is because the men love the scones so much or that I love to hear their prayers and concerns for our community, but I keep making them. It is an occasion that I never want to miss.

1 quart ice water
1 5-pound box biscuit mix
1 cup sugar
2 cups raisins or currants
½ teaspoon nutmeg
3 tablespoons lemon extract
2 eggs
½ cup milk
   Sugar

Preheat oven to 450°. In large mixing bowl, pour in ice water, making sure no ice remains. Add biscuit mix, sugar, raisins, nutmeg and lemon extract. Mix with electric mixer on low speed for two minutes, scraping sides often to blend well. Roll dough onto a floured board to form an 8x30-inch rectangle. Cut dough into 2-inch squares (60); cut squares into little triangles (120). Place triangles on buttered baking sheets. Whisk eggs and milk together. Brush over scones. Sprinkle heavily with sugar. Bake for 7 to 10 minutes or until golden brown. Serve hot.
   Makes 120 scones.

Laura Harper

▪ *Spoon Rolls* ▪

These are wonderful to have when company comes. Simply spoon the batter into muffin tins. The rolls will taste as if you've let them rise for hours.

1 package dry yeast
2 cups warm water
½ cup sugar
1½ sticks margarine, melted
1 egg, beaten
4 cups all-purpose flour

Dissolve yeast in water. In large bowl, cream sugar and margarine. Add egg and yeast mixture. Stir in flour until well mixed. Place dough in airtight container not more than ⅔ full. Refrigerate 1 to 2 hours before baking. Preheat oven to 350°. Drop by spoonsful into well-greased muffin tins. Bake for 20 minutes or until golden brown.

Note: This dough keeps for days in the refrigerator. Stir down lightly before using. Rolls are even better if the dough has seasoned for a day or two.

Makes 2½ dozen rolls.

Addie Tucker

▪ *Magnificent Rolls* ▪

The name says it all! We love these rolls and I have been making them for more than fifty years. It was my mother's recipe.

1 stick butter
½ cup sugar
1 8-ounce carton sour cream
1 teaspoon salt
2 packages dry yeast
½ cup warm water (110°)
2 teaspoons sugar
4 cups all-purpose flour
2 eggs, lightly beaten
1 egg white, whisked until foamy

Place butter into small saucepan over low heat. Slowly melt butter without browning; add ½ cup sugar, sour cream and salt. Set aside to cool while mixing the next ingredients. In a medium mixing bowl, dissolve yeast in warm water; add two teaspoons of sugar to activate yeast. Allow yeast to begin to foam and bubble while measuring flour. Measure flour into large mixing bowl. Make a hole in the center; add yeast and eggs. Before stirring, add sour cream mixture. Stir gradually; mix well. Dough should be soft—not a tight ball (add a little extra flour—up to ½ cup, if needed). Cover bowl with plastic wrap or foil, and place in refrigerator for about 8 hours or overnight. Remove from refrigerator; punch dough down. Pinch off dough about the size of a golf ball, flatten with palm of hand and then fold dough over to form a half circle. Place on buttered baking sheet. Cover and let rise in warm place for 1 hour (rolls should double in bulk). Preheat oven to 375°. Brush whisked egg white over tops of rolls. Bake for 10 to 12 minutes or until golden brown.

Makes 3 to 4 dozen rolls.

Dorothy Overstreet

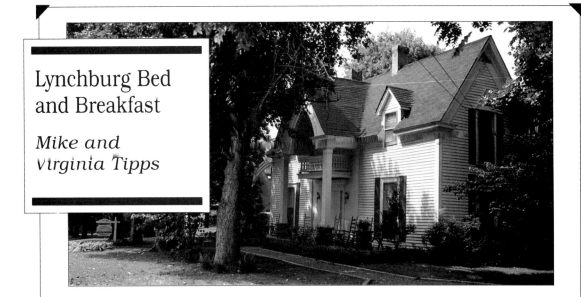

Lynchburg Bed and Breakfast

Mike and Virginia Tipps

To own a beautiful old Southern home built in 1877 by Moore County's first sheriff is a dream come true for Mike and Virginia Tipps. They live there with their two sons, Greg and Chad. Since they enjoy their home so much, they like to share it with visitors by running it as a bed and breakfast. A lovely, large home with giant shade trees in the front yard, a porch with old-fashioned Tennessee rockers on it, and antique-filled bedrooms make this a delight for guests.

Mike was born and reared in Lynchburg. Virginia was born in Manchester, about seventeen miles down the road. Both of them were working for the Jack Daniel Distillery when friends were transferred and had to sell their home. Virginia had been reading about the popularity of bed and breakfasts and wanted to try her hand at running her own business. Mike supported her idea because he knew that if enthusiasm could get the job done, Virginia could do it. They bought the house and the bed and breakfast opened.

Virginia is a friendly, cheerful, and happy hostess. She has had fun fixing up the rooms for overnight guests, buying quilts, furnishings, and accessories. She says, however, that the real enjoyment is in meeting those who have stayed there. The guest book shows that people have come from all over the world, and many keep in touch through letters and postcards.

Mornings find Virginia delivering big trays with cold juice, steaming hot coffee, and baskets of fresh-from-the-oven muffins (some of these recipes she shared with us). In this small town, the Lynchburg Bed and Breakfast is a first-class inn with friendly people who greet their guests and make them feel at home.

▪ *Buttermilk Yeast Rolls* ▪

4½ cups all-purpose flour, divided
3 tablespoons sugar
1 teaspoon salt
2 packages dry yeast
1¼ cups buttermilk
½ teaspoon baking soda
½ cup water
1 stick butter
  Extra melted butter

Combine 1½ cups flour, sugar, salt and yeast in large mixing bowl; set aside. Combine buttermilk, soda, water and 1 stick butter in small pan; heat to very warm (120°), stirring gently. Add to flour mixture; beat with mixer for 4 minutes. Gradually add remaining flour and continue to mix well. Turn dough onto a floured board; knead until smooth and elastic (at least 5 minutes). Cover and let rise in a warm place for about 30 minutes or until doubled in bulk. Punch dough down; shape into flat 2-inch circles. Dip in melted butter and fold top over; place on greased baking sheet. Cover and let rise again for 30 minutes or until doubled in bulk. Preheat oven to 400°. Bake rolls for about 20 minutes or until golden brown. Brush again with melted butter; serve hot.
  Makes 2 dozen rolls.

▪ *Crescent Rolls* ▪

Homemade bread is the best thing I know to make a plain dinner special. These are so good that my family wants only rolls with lots of butter and homemade preserves.

5 cups all-purpose flour, divided
¼ cup sugar
2 packages dry yeast
2 teaspoons salt
1 cup water
¾ cup milk
¼ cup vegetable oil
1 egg
1½ sticks butter, softened

Combine 1 cup flour, sugar, yeast and salt in a large bowl. Combine water, milk and oil in saucepan and heat to very warm (120°). Blend into flour mixture, using electric mixer. Add egg and mix for 5 minutes. Cut butter into remaining flour with fingertips or use pastry cutter (flour will resemble coarse corn meal). Combine the two flour mixtures; blend well. Place dough in greased bowl turning once to grease top. Cover; chill 2 hours. Punch dough down; turn out onto floured board. Knead 4 to 5 times. Divide dough into 4 equal balls. Roll each ball out on floured board to form a ¼-inch thick circle. Cut into wedges. Roll each wedge up beginning with the wide end to form a tight roll. Place rolls on a greased baking sheet with the point against the pan. Cover and let rise in a warm place until doubled in bulk (about 30 minutes). Preheat oven to 400°. Bake for approximately 20 minutes or until golden brown.
  Makes 3 dozen.

Diane Overstreet

• Six-Week Muffins •

1 cup solid shortening
3 cups sugar
4 eggs
5 cups unbleached and sifted all-
purpose flour
5 teaspoons baking soda
2 teaspoons salt
1 quart buttermilk
1 15-ounce package raisin bran

Preheat oven to 375°. Cream shortening and sugar; set aside. In separate bowl, lightly beat eggs. Mix 1 cup flour into the egg mixture. Add shortening mixture. Add remaining flour, soda and salt. Alternately mix dry ingredients with milk. Fold in bran. Place desired amount of dough into greased muffin cups. Bake for 15 to 20 minutes or until golden brown. Dough will keep well in refrigerator for 6 weeks. Baked muffins freeze well.
Makes 4 dozen.

Marie Cundall

• Sandy's Special Muffins •

2¼ cups oat bran
1 teaspoon ground cinnamon
1 tablespoon baking powder
¼ cup skim milk
¼ cup Jack Daniel's Whiskey
2 tablespoons vegetable oil
2 egg whites
¾ cup frozen apple juice
concentrate, thawed
¼ cup light corn syrup
½ cup applesauce
½ cup chopped pecans
½ cup raisins

Preheat oven to 425°. In a mixing bowl, combine first three ingredients; set aside. In a large bowl, combine milk, Jack Daniel's Whiskey, oil, egg whites, juice concentrate, corn syrup and applesauce. Blend well. Combine with the dry ingredients. Fold in pecans and raisins. Line a muffin tin with paper liners; fill with batter. Bake for 20 minutes or until golden brown. The longer the muffins cool, the easier they are to remove from the paper muffin cups.
Makes 1 dozen regular-size muffins.

Sandy Young

• Blueberry Muffins •

3 cups all-purpose flour
1 cup sugar
4 teaspoons baking powder
1 teaspoon salt
2 eggs, lightly beaten
½ cup vegetable oil
1 cup milk
1½ cups blueberries

Preheat oven to 400°. Mix flour, sugar, baking powder and salt in a bowl. Combine the eggs and oil; add the milk and stir into the dry ingredients just until moistened. Gently stir the blueberries into the mixture. Spoon into greased muffin cups filling each ½ full. Bake for 20 minutes. *Note:* Served at the Lynchburg Bed and Breakfast, the only place within the city limits where you can spend the night (Lynchburg has no hotels or motels).
Makes 14 large muffins.

Virginia Tipps

Baseball has become an event that is celebrated throughout the world. Televised games fill long afternoons for people everywhere, but in Lynchburg the homefolk gather at the park or the old schoolhouse where they participate as well as watch. Old-time fun like this is celebration enough for a long summer afternoon.

■ *Pineapple Dandy Muffins* ■

1⅔ cups sifted all-purpose flour
2 teaspoons baking powder
½ teaspoon salt
⅔ cup sugar
1 egg
⅓ cup vegetable oil
⅔ cup milk
⅓ cup crushed pineapple, drained

Preheat oven to 400°. Sift together flour, baking powder and salt. Add sugar, egg, oil, milk and pineapple. Mix just until flour is moistened. Batter will be lumpy. Fill each greased muffin cup ½ full. Bake for 20 to 25 minutes or until golden brown.
Makes 12 large muffins.

Virginia Tipps

■ *Double Cheese Apple Muffins* ■

1½ cups all-purpose flour
½ cup yellow cornmeal
½ cup diced dried apples
¼ cup packed brown sugar
1 tablespoon baking powder
¾ teaspoon cinnamon
1 cup milk
2 eggs, beaten
½ cup cream-style cottage cheese
½ stick butter, melted
½ cup shredded cheddar cheese

Preheat oven to 400°. Combine flour, cornmeal, apples, sugar, baking powder and cinnamon in a large mixing bowl. Combine milk, eggs, cottage cheese and butter in a small mixing bowl. Stir liquid ingredients into dry ingredients just until combined. Stir in cheddar cheese. Fill each buttered 2¾-inch muffin cup ⅔ full. Bake 20 to 25 minutes, or until skewer inserted in center comes out clean. Cool 5 minutes. Remove muffins from pans and cool slightly on wire rack.
Makes 12 muffins.

54

▪ *Oat-Banana Nut Muffins* ▪

This is a recipe that I found in a magazine. I don't recall the name of the magazine, but I have made some alterations in the ingredients of the recipe. I frequently serve a continental breakfast, and muffins and sweet breads are on the menu, along with coffee, tea and juice.

1½ cups all-purpose flour
1 cup regular oatmeal
½ cup sugar
1 teaspoon baking soda
⅛ teaspoon salt
⅓ cup chopped pecans or walnuts
1 egg, slightly beaten
½ cup mashed ripe banana (one medium)
¾ cup milk, whole or low fat
⅓ cup vegetable oil

Preheat oven to 400°. In large bowl, stir together dry ingredients. Add nuts and mix well; set aside. In small bowl, mix egg, banana, milk and oil until light and fluffy. Add liquid mixture all at once to dry ingredients, stirring just until moistened. Spoon batter into greased muffin cups filling each ⅔ full. Bake for 15 to 18 minutes. Cool 30 to 60 seconds in muffin pan; remove from pan. Paper liners can be used, but they tend to soften the outer crust.
Makes 1 dozen muffins.

Harriet Walsh-Rothfeldt

▪ *Country Sausage Muffins* ▪

½ pound bulk pork sausage
1 cup all-purpose flour
1 cup self-rising cornmeal
1 2-ounce jar diced pimiento, drained
1 8-ounce carton French onion dip
½ cup milk

Brown sausage, stirring to crumble. Drain well; reserve 2 tablespoons drippings. Preheat oven to 425°. Combine flour, cornmeal, sausage and pimiento; add reserved drippings, onion dip and milk. Stir. Fill each greased muffin cup ⅔ full. Bake for 20 to 25 minutes or until golden brown.
Makes 1 dozen.

Virginia Tipps

▪ *Sweetened Cornpone* ▪

4 cups cornmeal
½ cup sugar
4 cups boiling water
½ cup molasses
1 egg, beaten
1½ cups all-purpose flour
1½ teaspoons baking soda
2 teaspoons baking powder
1 cup buttermilk

Mix cornmeal, sugar and boiling water together until smooth. Let stand overnight in a tightly covered container in a warm place. When ready to bake, preheat oven to 450°. Add remaining ingredients to cornmeal mixture; mix well. Pour into a greased cast-iron skillet. Bake at 450° for 15 minutes; reduce heat to 350° and bake for 45 minutes longer. Remove from oven; wrap in towel until ready to slice.
Makes 6 to 8 servings.

▪ *Hush Puppy Hoe Cakes* ▪

4 cups cornmeal
1 teaspoon salt
Boiling water
Shortening
Butter

Mix cornmeal and salt. Add enough boiling water to make a stiff batter. Moisten hands with cold water. Take enough batter to pat into a cake about 2 inches in diameter. Fry in about ½-inch deep shortening in a cast-iron skillet. Brown on one side; turn to brown other. Serve hot with butter. Especially good with a pot of beans instead of regular cornbread.
Makes 16 servings.

Debbie Mitchamore

▪ *Sweet Potato Corn Bread* ▪

3 eggs
2½ cups sweet potatoes, cooked and mashed
2 sticks butter, softened
1½ cups cornmeal
½ cup all-purpose flour
1 teaspoon baking soda
1 teaspoon baking powder
Buttermilk

Preheat oven to 400°. Mix eggs into sweet potatoes. Beat in butter. Gradually add remaining ingredients using enough buttermilk for a good consistency. Pour into a greased 10-inch cast-iron skillet. Bake for about 30 minutes or until golden brown and firm in center.
Makes 6 servings.

▪ *Johnnycakes* ▪

1 cup cornmeal
½ cup sifted all-purpose flour
2 tablespoons sugar
1½ teaspoons baking powder
1 teaspoon salt
1 egg, beaten
1¼ cups milk
Butter
Syrup

Sift together cornmeal, flour, sugar, baking powder and salt. Add beaten egg and milk; blend thoroughly. For each Johnnycake, pour a scant ¼ cup batter onto a hot, lightly greased griddle. Cook to a golden brown, turning only once. Serve with butter and syrup.
Makes 4 servings.

Viola Mitchamore

▪ *Corn Muffins or Corn Sticks* ▪

1 cup all-purpose flour
3 teaspoons baking powder
1 teaspoon salt
1 cup milk
1 egg
1 cup cornmeal
⅓ cup sugar
½ stick butter, melted

Preheat oven to 425°. Sift together flour, baking powder and salt. Mix in milk and egg; stir in cornmeal. Add remaining ingredients; blend well. Pour into well-greased pan. Bake for about 20 minutes or until golden brown. This can also be baked in an 8-inch square pan and cut into squares.

Makes 6 servings.

Norma Rigler

▪ *Sour Cream Cornbread* ▪

This is a good cornbread to serve with fresh vegetables.

1 cup self-rising cornmeal
2 eggs
1 8-ounce carton sour cream
1 8¾-ounce can cream-style corn
¼ cup vegetable oil, divided

Preheat oven to 350°. Combine cornmeal, eggs, sour cream and corn; mix thoroughly. Pour half the oil into an 8-inch skillet and heat. Add the remaining oil to the batter. Pour batter into hot skillet. Bake for 25 to 30 minutes or until golden brown.

Makes 6 servings.

Bobbie Payne

▪ *Quick and Easy Hush Puppies* ▪

1 cup self-rising cornmeal
½ cup self-rising flour
1 tablespoon sugar
1 egg
1 medium onion, finely chopped
½ green pepper, finely chopped (or
   1 jalapeño pepper)
1 cup milk
   Vegetable oil

Combine cornmeal, flour, sugar, egg, onion, pepper and milk. Drop by tablespoonsful into hot (370°) oil. Fry until golden brown on all sides. Drain on paper towels.

Makes about 2 dozen.

Carroll Harris

· ENTRÉES ·

The main dish of a meal is like the main event at a celebration: it is what everyone is waiting for. This is what all the side attractions are supposed to enhance. Nothing captures the moment like the entrée.

History shows us that main dishes often reflect the times. During the Great Depression "chicken every Sunday" was the ultimate mark of well being. After World War II came a period of abundant food and lavish meals. Not only was plenty of food available, but we wanted to reward ourselves for sacrifices made during the war.

Today the trend is to eat dishes that are light and healthy. Many people are jogging, walking, or biking. Discussing fat, salt intake, and cholesterol levels makes conversation and eating healthful meals popular.

With the emphasis on the lower fat meats such as fish and poultry, we see lots of ways to prepare these dishes. But we can also indulge ourselves occasionally, and so other favorites are included here, proving again that the main event is worth waiting for.

▪ *Chicken Pot Pie* ▪

This recipe came from my daughter in Amarillo, Texas. While I was helping her when she had her second child she asked me to make Chicken Pot Pie for dinner. She gave me the following recipe. It can be made early in the day and refrigerated. Just add 5 to 10 minutes to the baking time.

1 16-ounce package frozen mixed vegetables
½ cup chopped fresh mushrooms, or 1 small can mushrooms will substitute
½ cup chopped onion
½ stick margarine
⅓ cup all-purpose flour
½ teaspoon salt
¼ teaspoon ground sage
⅛ teaspoon white or black pepper
2 cups water, or chicken broth from simmered chicken
¾ cup milk
1 tablespoon instant chicken bouillon granules
3 cups cubed, cooked chicken (use 1 2- to 3-pound chicken simmered with celery)
¼ cup chopped pimiento
¼ cup snipped fresh parsley
  Pastry for double crust pie

Cook mixed vegetables according to package directions; drain. In a saucepan, cook mushrooms and onion in margarine until tender but not brown. Stir in flour, salt, sage and pepper. Add water or broth (which makes a tastier gravy), milk, and chicken bouillon granules all at once. Cook and stir until thickened and bubbly. Simmer and stir for 1 to 2 minutes. Stir in vegetables, chicken, pimiento and parsley. Heat until bubbly. Preheat oven to 450°. Turn chicken mixture into a 12x7½-inch baking dish. Roll pastry into a 13x9-inch rectangle; place over casserole and flute edges. Cut slits in top for steam to escape. Bake for 10 to 12 minutes or until crust is brown. Premade refrigerated all-ready pie crust also works great.

Note: This recipe can be doubled for a larger pie. Corn bread or corn sticks, plus a layered salad or carrot salad goes great to complete the meal.

Makes 4 to 6 servings, depending on appetites.

Harriet Walsh-Rothfeldt

▪ *Easy Chicken Tetrazzini* ▪

1 pound fresh mushrooms, sliced
1 clove garlic, minced
2 tablespoons melted butter
1 teaspoon salt
⅛ teaspoon pepper
¼ teaspoon thyme
2 cups cooked, diced chicken or turkey
1 10½-ounce can cream of celery soup
1 8-ounce carton sour cream
1 8-ounce package spaghetti or noodles
½ cup grated Parmesan cheese

Sauté mushrooms and garlic in butter in large skillet. Add salt, pepper, thyme, chicken, soup and sour cream; mix well. Cook spaghetti according to package directions; drain. Preheat over to 375°. Layer spaghetti and chicken mixture in a greased 13x9-inch baking dish. Sprinkle with cheese. Bake for 25 minutes.

Makes 6 servings.

Lynne Farrar

■ *Moody Ranch Chicken* ■

This recipe is a variation of the famous King Ranch Chicken, a South-western favorite. It is perfect for large dinner parties and it freezes well.

My grandparents, Mr. and Mrs. Denman Moody have a beautiful ranch outside of Rocksprings, Texas. The ranch has been in our family for several generations and is the gathering place for our loved ones during all holidays. We have enjoyed many wonderful times at the ranch, and we all look forward to the fantastic food served during the holiday weekends. One of our favorite dishes is Moody Ranch Chicken, a delicious blend of chicken, cheeses and peppers.

When I moved to Nashville, Tennessee, I wanted to have a few of my new friends over for supper. I consulted with a Texas friend about what I should prepare. She advised me to make a dish that would be representative of my home state, so of course, I made Moody Ranch Chicken. It was such a hit that I have had to make it for almost every dinner party I have given since because all my friends love it so much.

1 large chicken
Salt and pepper to taste
1 10¾-ounce can cream of mushroom soup
1 10¾-ounce can cream of chicken soup
1 small onion, chopped
1 10-ounce can Rotel tomatoes and green chilies, drained
1 8-ounce jar Cheez Whiz
1 11-ounce bag of Doritos, crushed (or any corn chip)
1 8-ounce package grated cheddar cheese
1 4-ounce package grated Mozzarella cheese

Boil chicken in enough water to cover with salt and pepper until tender. Debone chicken and chop into bite-size pieces; set aside. In a large saucepan, over medium heat mix soups, onion, Rotel tomatoes and Cheez Whiz until blended. Preheat oven to 350°. Layer bottom of a greased 9x12-inch casserole dish with Doritos. Next, layer half the chicken pieces. Top with half the sauce. Sprinkle half the cheddar cheese on top. Repeat layers. Top with remaining cheddar and Mozzarella cheeses. Bake for 30 to 45 minutes or until hot and bubbly throughout.

Makes 6 to 8 servings.

Teddy Heard Orr

■ *Lemon Chicken* ■

The Pieroni family in Ancona, Italy has passed down this recipe for generations. Now it has made it to the New World and it is still delicious!

1 chicken, cut into pieces
¼ cup olive oil
8 cloves garlic, crushed
Juice of 8 lemons
2 cups finely chopped parsley
Salt and pepper to taste

Sauté chicken pieces in olive oil until browned. Add garlic, lemon juice and parsley; stir gently to combine. Sprinkle with salt and pepper. Cover; turn heat to low. Cook for 1 hour or until tender.

Makes 6 to 8 servings.

Cecilia Lucchesi

61

These cooks are famous all over the country and in many places around the world. Every day except Sunday they cook up an old-fashioned boarding house mid-day dinner. It is a celebration of the past, food served family-style at big tables for twelve. Fried chicken, hot rolls, fresh vegetables, and pies from their kitchen make eating dinner at Mary Bobo's a prized experience.

▪ *Chicken with Doodle Soup* ▪

Dot Elam of Lynchburg has been cooking this for years. Her husband, Rudy, has fond memories of his grandmother (Jo Eddie Elam) hanging a hen by a string in front of the fireplace in her kitchen when he was a child. The string was twisted so that it turned and let the hen cook evenly. It was his job to keep the string twisted so that it would turn. A pan was placed underneath the hen to catch the drippings. The hen was basted with pepper juice from home-canned cayenne peppers. They always served the hen with crackers and Doodle Soup.

1 cup vinegar
1 cup water
2 teaspoons salt
1 tablespoon crushed red pepper
½ teaspoon black pepper
1 5 to 6-pound hen
2 cups water

Combine first 5 ingredients in saucepan. Bring to a boil; set aside. Preheat oven to 350°. Salt and pepper hen. Place on a trivet in a covered baking pan. Add 2 cups of water. Roast for 3 hours or until nice and brown and well done. During the cooking, baste with vinegar sauce.

Doodle Soup: When hen is done, pour drippings into a saucepan and cook down. If not spicy enough, add some of the vinegar sauce. To serve, carve the hen and serve alongside a basket of saltine crackers. You crush several crackers on your plate and use the Doodle Soup as a gravy, if you like.

Makes 4 to 6 servings.

Dot Elam

Miss Mary Bobo's Boarding House

The bounty of a meal served family-style is an experience of pure joy. In this day of fast foods, finger foods, and instant potatoes on TV trays, family-style serving is an endangered tradition. Unfortunately, generous serving bowls of creamed potatoes, beans with ham hocks, fried corn, squash or broccoli casserole, platters of chicken, pork chops, pot roast, and homemade bread may go the way of the washboard, lye soap, and wringer washers!

Boarding houses were always known for their family-style service because their tables were laden with delectable dishes. A room in a good boarding house was a treasure and because of the food served, envied by those not so fortunate. This delight of the past can still be enjoyed in Lynchburg, the home of Miss Mary Bobo's Boarding House, established in 1908.

In celebration of all these old estab-lishments and in particular the one run by Mary Bobo and her husband, Jack, Lynne Tolley and her staff serve a boarding house meal there every day except July 4, Christmas, and New Year's. Among the foods served to the guests are fried chicken, okra, grits, sweet potatoes, fresh-from-the-garden corn, beans, cabbage, tomatoes, hot breads, and scrumptious desserts. Diners from various parts of the country are seated together like family groups with a Lynchburg hostess at every table. Second helpings or thirds are encouraged.

The same cooks who have been pre-paring these dishes for many years are still in the kitchen cooking things the old-fashioned way, using iron skillets for chicken, real meringue for pies, and fresh-picked vegetables. Here is a tradi-tional food celebration for everyone. We invite you to come and enjoy!

■ *Lemon-Dill Chicken* ■

4 chicken breasts
4 teaspoons butter
1 lemon, thinly sliced
2 teaspoons dill weed
  Salt and pepper to taste

Preheat oven to 300°. Make four aluminum foil squares. Place one chicken breast in each square. On each chicken breast, place 1 teaspoon butter, 2 thin slices lemon, ½ teaspoon dill weed, salt and pepper. Fold foil packets to seal. Bake for 1 hour. This is a delicious low-calorie meal when served with brown rice and tossed salad.

Makes 4 servings.

Kathy Scheib

■ *Poppy Seed Chicken* ■

Great to carry to church dinners. Good with a large tossed salad!

4 to 5 chicken breasts
2 chicken bouillon cubes
1 8-ounce carton sour cream
1 10¾-ounce can cream of chicken
  soup
20 Ritz crackers
1 stick butter, melted
  Poppy seed

Boil chicken breasts with bouillon cubes and enough water to cover until tender. Debone and tear into small pieces. Line bottom of greased casserole dish with chicken pieces. Preheat oven to 350°. Mix together sour cream and soup. Spread over chicken. Crumble crackers over mixture. Pour melted butter over crackers. Sprinkle poppy seed over top. Bake for about 20 minutes or until bubbly.

Makes 4 to 5 servings.

Sara Wood

■ *Crock Pot Chicken in White Wine* ■

4 chicken breasts or 1 whole
  chicken
1 cup white cooking wine
⅓ cup soy sauce
½ teaspoon thyme
½ teaspoon sage
½ teaspoon coarsely ground pepper
2 potatoes, unpeeled and cut into
  chunks
2 carrots, cut into chunks
1 stalk celery, cut into chunks
1 onion, cut into chunks
1 green pepper, cut into chunks,
  optional

Place all ingredients in crock pot. Be sure liquid covers all, add ½ cup water if needed, to cover. Set crock pot on low; cook for 8 to 12 hours. Delicious and easy working woman's meal.

Makes 4 servings

Kathy Scheib

64

▪ Chicken Quiche ▪

3 eggs
1 1.25-ounce package chicken gravy
¾ cup cooked, cubed chicken
1 cup milk
  Pastry for 9-inch deep-dish pie
1 8-ounce package shredded Swiss cheese

Preheat oven to 350°. Beat eggs; blend in gravy mix, chicken and milk. Pour into deep dish pie crust. Sprinkle Swiss cheese over top. Bake for 30 to 40 minutes or until brown and firm in the center.

Makes 4 to 6 servings.

Judy Heslar

▪ Brunswick Stew ▪

1 1½- to 2-pound fryer, cut into pieces
1 tablespoon salt, divided
  Paprika to taste
½ stick butter
2 medium onions, sliced
1 medium green pepper, diced
3 cups water
2 cups canned tomatoes, chopped
2 tablespoons chopped parsley
½ teaspoon hot pepper sauce
1 teaspoon Worcestershire sauce
2 cups whole kernel corn
1 10-ounce package frozen lima beans
3 tablespoons all-purpose flour

Sprinkle chicken with 1 teaspoon salt and paprika. Heat butter in a large saucepan or Dutch oven; add chicken and brown on all sides. Add onion and green pepper; cook until onion is transparent. Add water, tomatoes, parsley, remaining salt, hot pepper sauce and Worcestershire sauce; bring to a boil. Cover; reduce heat, simmer for 30 minutes. Add corn and lima beans; cook 20 minutes longer. Blend flour with a little cold water; gradually stir into stew. Cook 10 minutes longer, stirring constantly until thickened.

Makes 8 servings.

Mary Cleeton

▪ Gourmet Baked Chicken ▪

5 whole chicken breasts, halved, boned and skinned
2 cups sour cream
1 tablespoon Worcestershire sauce
2 teaspoons salt
1¼ teaspoons paprika
1¼ cups fine bread crumbs
  Melted butter

Wash chicken; pat dry with paper towels. Place in shallow baking dish. Combine sour cream, Worcestershire sauce, salt and paprika; pour over chicken. Turn chicken to coat. Cover and refrigerate overnight. Drop chicken pieces, one at a time, into bread crumbs, turning to coat. Shape each piece to make a nice round fillet. Place in buttered baking dish. Preheat oven to 325°. Bake, uncovered, for 1¼ hours or until tender and golden. While baking, if chicken begins to dry, baste with a little melted butter.

Makes 10 servings.

Susanna Kane

• *Turkey Pot Pie* •

1 26-ounce package assorted
   frozen vegetables
1½ cups water
 2 10¾-ounce cans cream of
   broccoli, potato or mushroom
   soup
 2 cups cubed turkey (chicken or
   beef can be substituted)
½ teaspoon dried thyme leaves
 2 cups biscuit mix
⅔ cup skim milk
 1 egg yolk, mixed with 1 teaspoon
   water

Boil vegetables in 1½ cups water until tender. Drain and reserve ¾ cup of liquid. Combine soups, reserved liquid, vegetables, turkey and thyme. Pour into a greased 3-quart oval casserole. Preheat oven to 350°. Combine biscuit mix and milk. Mix well; turn onto floured surface. Knead, flatten and roll out. Cover top of vegetables and cut a plus sign in the center. Fold back cut edges. Brush with egg yolk. Bake for 30 minutes or until browned and bubbly.
Makes 8 servings.

Mrs. Jerry Dickey

• *New York Jack* •

I'm a chef at the Silver Lining Restaurant at the Arcata/Eureka Airport in California. While trying to think of a "special" for the day, I thought of using Jack Daniel's Whiskey in a cream sauce over New York strip steak.

2 to 3 tablespoons clarified butter
1 12-ounce New York strip steak
½ cup sliced mushrooms
3 to 4 tablespoons Jack Daniel's
   Whiskey
½ cup heavy cream

Heat butter in skillet over medium-high heat. Sear steak on one side. Add mushrooms. Sear steak on second side while browning mushrooms. Remove meat from pan; keep warm. Flambé pan with Jack Daniel's Whiskey. When flame burns out, add cream. Stir until thickened. Pour sauce over steak to serve.
Makes 1 serving.

Sean Aragon

• *Country-Style Steak* •

1 pound round steak
1 teaspoon Adolph's seasoned
   meat tenderizer
1 cup all-purpose flour
¼ teaspoon black pepper
   Vegetable oil
1 cup water
1 10¾-ounce can cream of
   mushroom soup

Cut steak into serving-size pieces. Combine meat tenderizer, flour and pepper. Dredge steak in flour mixture. Heat 1-inch deep oil in a heavy skillet to cover steak. Place steak in hot oil; brown on both sides. Remove steak from oil; drain oil from skillet. Add water and soup and stir until smooth. Add the steak; cover and simmer on low heat for 1 hour. More water may be added, if needed.
Makes 4 servings.

Served at Miss Mary Bobo's Boarding House

Whether it's a fair, a holiday, or a backyard get-together, cookouts are big in every hometown. Barbecuing and grilling have been referred to as the great American pastime, and here in Lynchburg there is no better way to pass the time than cooking and eating outside.

▪ Braised Sirloin Tips ▪

1½ pounds mushrooms, sliced
½ stick butter, divided
1 tablespoon vegetable oil
1 3-pound sirloin steak, cut into 1 inch cubes
¾ cup beef bouillon
¾ cup red wine
2 tablespoons soy sauce
2 cloves garlic, minced
½ onion, grated
2 tablespoons cornstarch
⅓ cup beef bouillon
Half a 10¾-ounce can cream of mushroom soup
Salt to taste
Hot cooked rice

Sauté mushrooms in 2 tablespoons butter until lightly browned; spoon into a greased 3-quart casserole. Add remaining butter and oil to skillet; add meat and brown on all sides. Spoon meat over mushrooms. Preheat oven to 275°. Combine ¾ cup bouillon, wine, soy sauce, garlic and onion; add to skillet, scraping bottom to blend all particles. Blend cornstarch with ⅓ cup bouillon; stir into wine mixture. Cook, stirring constantly, until smooth and thickened. Spoon over meat; stir to mix. Cover and bake for 1 hour. Add mushroom soup, stirring until smooth. Add salt to taste. Bake 15 minutes longer. Serve over cooked rice.

Makes 8 servings.

Caroline Heard

▪ Chinese Pepper Steak ▪

This is the best stretch steak recipe that I know. The only thing is you have to have lots of it because it is so good people eat twice as much. I first cooked this in the '50s and after each of my children got married this was the first recipe they asked for. It's easy and delicious!

1 envelope dry onion soup mix
1½ cups boiling water
4 tablespoons vegetable oil
1 clove garlic
1 pound round steak, cut in pieces or strips
All-purpose flour
1 tablespoon soy sauce
2 green peppers, cut into strips
1 tablespoon cornstarch
3 tablespoons cold water
Hot cooked rice, noodles or mashed potatoes

Combine soup mix and boiling water, set aside. Heat oil in large skillet. Sauté garlic in oil; remove garlic and discard. Roll steak strips in flour. Brown meat quickly in oil over high heat. Add soup mixture, soy sauce and peppers. Blend cornstarch in cold water. Pour over meat mixture. Cover and cook over low heat until tender. Serve over rice or noodles or use mashed potatoes as a side dish. (Double gravy if using potatoes).

Makes 4 to 6 servings.

Dorothy Overstreet

67

■ *The Working Person's Roast* ■

The following recipe is one that I use frequently and is one of my favorites.

1 roast (can be beef or pork, expensive cuts do not taste better than inexpensive ones; size is determined by need)
1 clove fresh garlic, slivered
1 10¾-ounce can cream of mushroom soup
2 tablespoons Worcestershire sauce
1 envelope Lipton's onion soup mix

Place the roast in center of large sheet of aluminum foil; cut slits in roast and push in garlic slivers. Pour mushroom soup over roast; pour Worcestershire sauce over soup. Sprinkle soup mix over top. Pull foil up and seal across top and ends; be sure it is sealed tightly, leaving space above and around roast. Place in pan and put in 250° oven from 7 a.m. to 5 p.m. Your roast is tender and juicy and it makes its own gravy. Enjoy.

Makes 6 to 8 servings.

Barbara Wright

■ *Herb-Stuffed Flank Steak with Tomato Whiskey Sauce* ■

This was the third prize winner of the 1988 Tennessee Beef Cook-Off!

1½ pounds flank steak, butterflied
2 cups soft bread crumbs
½ stick butter
1 small onion, chopped
1 teaspoon each chervil, sage, tarragon, basil, cilantro and black pepper
1 15-ounce can herb tomato sauce
½ cup Jack Daniel's Whiskey

Butterfly steak by slicing along the grain of the steak, cutting carefully so the steak will lay flat. Prepare bread crumbs by placing slices of white bread in food processor or by using a hand grater. Melt butter in small skillet; sauté onion in butter for 3 or 4 minutes. Combine onion, herbs and bread crumbs. Spread herb-crumb mixture over flank steak to within 1 inch of sides. Roll up jelly-roll style across the steak. Tie with a string and place in dish to marinate. Mix tomato sauce and Jack Daniel's Whiskey. Pour over prepared steak and chill several hours or overnight. Preheat oven to 325°. Transfer steak to baking dish. Bake for 1½ to 2 hours. Remove from pan and cool 20 minutes before slicing. Slice across the grain making 8 equal slices. Serve heated sauce in separate dish.

Makes 4 servings (2 slices each).

Barbara Jones

68

When harvest comes, farmers take their fresh produce to the farmer's market. Freshly picked fruits and vegetables are displayed so that all may enjoy their color and beauty.

▪ Legendary Chili ▪

5 pounds ground chili meat (don't get lean meat—meat needs to have fat in it for flavor)
1 large onion, chopped
2 1.25-ounce packages taco seasoning mix
2 1.25-ounce packages chili seasoning mix
2 15-ounce cans tomato sauce
1 8-ounce jar mild picante sauce
2 16-ounce cans chili hot beans
¼ cup Jack Daniel's Whiskey
   Small bags of corn chips

In a large Dutch oven cook ground meat, stirring to keep meat loose. When meat is almost done, add onion; cook, stirring often, until meat is gray and onions are glazed. Skim grease from top constantly. Stir in taco and chili mix seasonings. Add tomato sauce, picante sauce and beans. Rinse cans with small amount of water and add to chili. Simmer 10 minutes. Add Jack Daniel's Whiskey and simmer 10 more minutes. To serve, use small packages of corn chips. Slit open top of bag. Spoon chili over chips. Pass out plastic spoons. Makes great chili for food bazaars.
   Makes 1 gallon.

▪ Cheeseburger Loaf ▪

1½ pounds lean ground chuck
1 10¾-ounce can condensed tomato soup, divided
1 egg
1 large onion, chopped
1 medium green pepper, chopped
1 cup cracker or bread crumbs
1½ teaspoons salt
½ teaspoon black pepper
1 cup cubed Velveeta cheese
½ cup water
½ cup chopped white potatoes, optional
6 slices American cheese

Preheat oven to 350°. Combine all ingredients, except half the tomato soup and American cheese. Mix well, form into loaf, and place in greased baking dish. Bake for 30 minutes. Remove from oven. Top with cheese slices. Mix the remaining soup with ¼ cup of water and pour over the cheese. Return to oven and bake an additional 30 minutes.
   Makes 8 servings.

James C. Murray

▪ *Beef Stroganoff* ▪

3 to 4 pounds round steak, cut
  into 1-inch strips
  Flour
1 stick butter
2 cloves garlic
2 3-ounce cans broiled-in-butter
  mushrooms, drained and liquid
  reserved
1 cup water
2 medium onions, chopped
2 10¾-ounce cans cream of
  mushroom soup
2 cups sour cream
¼ cup catsup
4 tablespoons Worcestershire
  sauce
  Dash of hot pepper sauce
  Hot cooked rice

Dredge meat in flour and brown in butter in large skillet (add extra butter as needed). Add garlic, liquid from mushrooms and 1 cup water. Cover and simmer for 1 hour (check occasionally adding more water if needed). Mix mushrooms, onion, soup, sour cream, catsup, Worcestershire and pepper sauces; add to meat. Cover and simmer for another hour. Serve over hot rice.

Makes 8 servings.

Thelma Grisham

▪ *No-Peek Stew* ▪

2 pounds lean stew meat
1 10¾-ounce can cream of
  mushroom soup
1 envelope onion soup mix or stew
  mix
1 cup water
  Buttered noodles or rice
  Poppy seed, optional

Preheat oven to 300°. Mix first 4 ingredients in a 13x9x2-inch casserole dish and cover with a tight lid or foil. Bake for 3 hours. No Peeking!! Serve with buttered noodles or rice. Sprinkle with poppy seed, if desired.

Makes 6 servings.

Mary Cleeton

▪ *Hungarian Goulash With Egg Noodles* ▪

1½ pounds onions, thinly sliced
3 tablespoons butter
1½ pounds cubed beef
1 tablespoon paprika
2 teaspoons salt
¼ teaspoon pepper
3 cups water
1 8-ounce package egg noodles
2 tablespoons poppy seed,
  optional

In a large saucepan, sauté onion in butter for about 5 minutes. Add beef, paprika, salt, pepper and water. Simmer, covered, 1½ to 2 hours or until meat is tender, stirring occasionally. Meanwhile, cook noodles as directed. Drain. Toss with poppy seed. Serve goulash over noodles.

Makes 4 servings.

Kathy Woodard

▪ *Plantation Supper* ▪

1 pound ground beef
½ cup chopped onion
¾ cup milk
1 10¾-ounce can cream of
  mushroom soup
1 8-ounce package cream cheese,
  cut into cubes
1½ cups whole kernel corn, drained
¼ cup chopped pimientos
1 8-ounce package noodles,
  cooked and drained
1½ teaspoons salt
  Dash of pepper

Preheat oven to 325°. Brown meat; add onion and cook until tender. Drain. Stir in milk, soup and cheese until well blended. Add remaining ingredients. Pour into a greased casserole. Bake for 85 minutes or until heated thoroughly and bubbling.
  Makes 6 servings.

Mrs. Melvin Metcalf

▪ *Jambalaya* ▪

3 cups water
1½ cups brown rice
  Dash of salt
1 tablespoon olive oil
1 onion, chopped
2 green peppers, chopped
3 stalks celery, chopped
1 teaspoon cayenne pepper
1 teaspoon black pepper
2 cups chicken broth
1 14½-ounce can chopped
  tomatoes
1 pound country ham, shredded
1 tablespoon thyme vinegar

Bring water to a boil in a heavy saucepan; add rice and salt. Stir once, turn heat to low. Cover with close-fitting lid; simmer for 45 minutes. When rice is ready, heat olive oil in a separate, large pan and sauté the onion, pepper and celery lightly—just enough to coat them with oil. Add the rice, spices, broth and tomatoes. Bring to a quick boil, then turn heat to simmer. Mix in ham and vinegar; let the flavors mingle on very low heat for at least 20 minutes. Stir occasionally to keep from sticking and add water as needed—the finished jambalaya should be thick, not soupy.
  Makes 6 servings.

Crystal Iglesias

▪ *Pork Chop Spanish Rice* ▪

5 pork chops
2 tablespoons solid shortening
1 teaspoon salt
½ teaspoon chili powder
  Dash of pepper
¾ cup uncooked long-grain rice
½ cup chopped onion
¼ cup chopped green pepper
1 12-ounce can tomatoes
5 green pepper rings
½ cup shredded sharp process
  American cheese

Trim excess fat from chops. Slowly brown chops in melted shortening; drain off excess fat. Combine salt, chili powder and pepper; sprinkle over meat. Add rice, onion and chopped green pepper; add tomatoes. Cover and cook over low heat for 35 minutes, stirring occasionally. Add green pepper rings; cook 5 minutes longer or until rice and meat are tender. Sprinkle with cheese before serving.
  Makes 5 servings.

Mary Edwards

71

▪ *Baked Ham With Raisin Sauce* ▪

1 honey-cured ham, fully cooked
  and smoked
½ cup packed light brown sugar
4 teaspoons cornstarch
¼ teaspoon ground cloves
¼ teaspoon ground cinnamon
1¼ cups orange juice
1 tablespoon lemon juice
½ cup golden seedless raisins

Preheat oven to 325°. Place ham fat-side up on rack in open roasting pan. Insert meat thermometer into center of thickest part of ham. Roast until meat thermometer registers 140°F., allowing 15 to 18 minutes per pound. To prepare raisin sauce, combine sugar, cornstarch, cloves and cinnamon in saucepan; add orange juice and lemon juice and stir until free of lumps. Add raisins. Cook over medium heat, stirring constantly, until sauce is thickened and boiling. Brush sauce over ham during last 20 minutes of cooking. Serve remaining sauce warm with ham.
  Makes 1⅔ cups sauce.

Ruby Hyde

Ham Glazes

If a glaze is desired, brush it on the ham ½ hour before the end of cooking time.

CHERRY HONEY GLAZE: Combine ¾ cup cherry preserves, ½ cup honey, ⅛ teaspoon ground cinnamon, ⅛ teaspoon allspice, ¼ teaspoon grated lemon rind and 2 tablespoons pineapple juice. Cook over medium heat, stirring constantly, until boiling. Brush ham 2 or 3 times during last 30 minutes of cooking time. Serve remaining glaze warm with ham. Makes about 1¼ cups.

BROWN SUGAR GLAZE: Stir together 1 cup packed brown sugar, ½ teaspoon ground cloves, 1 teaspoon dry mustard, ¼ cup pineapple juice and 1 tablespoon lemon juice. Makes ¾ cup.

PINEAPPLE-ORANGE GLAZE: Mix together ½ cup pineapple preserves, 1½ teaspoons cornstarch, 1 teaspoon grated orange peel, ⅛ teaspoon ground cinnamon, ⅛ teaspoon ground cloves and ¼ cup orange juice. Cook over medium heat, stirring constantly, until thickened and boiling. Makes ¾ cup.

PINEAPPLE GLAZE: Mix 1 cup packed light brown sugar, ⅛ teaspoon ground cloves, ⅛ teaspoon allspice, 2 tablespoons cornstarch, 1 8½-ounce can crushed pineapple, 2 tablespoons lemon juice and 1 tablespoon prepared mustard. Cook over medium heat, stirring constantly, until mixture thickens and boils; reduce heat and cook about 2 minutes. Brush glaze over ham 2 or 3 times during last 30 minutes of cooking time. Serve remaining glaze warm with ham. Makes 1½ cups.

▪ *Pork Chops And Gravy* ▪

This main dish makes its own gravy and is especially good with rice and English peas.

2 to 3 pounds center-cut pork
   chops
   Flour
   Salt and pepper to taste
4 tablespoons vegetable oil
2 medium onions, sliced
1 10¾-ounce can cream of
   mushroom soup

Preheat oven to 000°. Dredge pork chops in flour and sprinkle with salt and pepper. Brown chops quickly in oil in skillet over high heat. Place chops in a 9x12-inch baking dish; cover with sliced onions. Add soup and ¾ cup water to drippings in skillet and stir until hot. Pour over pork chop mixture. Cover pan with foil. Bake for 1½ hours.

Makes 6 servings.

Mrs. Lilbern Rutledge

▪ *Seafood Au Gratin* ▪

This is a delicious sauce to use with your favorite seafood—shrimp, lobster, crab or scallops. Serve it over rice or for a lip-smacking treat. Toast slices of French bread and top with spoonfuls of gratin sauce—garnish with a sprinkle of paprika and a sprig of parsley—a real party dish!

2 cups finely chopped onion
2 cups finely chopped celery
1 clove garlic, minced
4 sticks butter, divided
1 cup all-purpose flour
2 cups milk
1 quart half-and-half, divided
½ pound Swiss cheese, shredded
1 teaspoon salt
   Fresh cracked pepper to taste
3 egg yolks
2 cups seafood
   Rice or French bread slices
   Bread crumbs
   Shredded cheddar cheese

Sauté onion, celery and garlic in heavy skillet in two sticks of butter. Add remaining butter. Mix flour in a small mixing bowl with cold milk, stirring rapidly to prevent lumps; add to onion mixture. Stir over low heat, being sure butter and sauce do not brown. Add 2 cups half-and-half, stirring to blend over low heat. Add Swiss cheese, stirring constantly until cheese melts. Add salt, pepper and remaining half-and-half; stir until thickened. Whisk egg yolks until thick and frothy; mix into sauce, stirring rapidly to blend well. Add your choice of seafood: 2 cans of lump crabmeat or 2 cups of cooked, cleaned and shelled shrimp or even 2 cans of drained albacore tuna. Stir to blend. Use individual gratin dishes layered with rice or toasted French bread. Spoon on sauce and top with a generous sprinkling of bread crumbs and shredded cheddar cheese. Place under broiler until cheese melts. Serve immediately.

Makes 8 servings.

■ *Classic Fried Catfish* ■

¾ cup cornmeal, yellow or white
¼ cup all-purpose flour
2 teaspoons salt
1 teaspoon cayenne pepper
¼ teaspoon garlic powder
4 catfish fillets (or whole)
  Vegetable oil

Combine cornmeal, flour, salt, cayenne pepper and garlic powder. Coat catfish with mixture; shake off excess. Fill deep pot or 12-inch skillet half full with vegetable oil.* Heat oil to 350°F. Add catfish in single layer; fry until golden brown, about 5 to 6 minutes, depending on size. Remove and drain on paper towels. *Variation:* For **Crispy Classic Fried Catfish,** combine ⅓ cup sour cream, ⅓ cup Dijon mustard and 3 tablespoons water in a separate shallow dish. (Prepare cornmeal mixture as above, omitting salt.) Dip catfish in sour cream mixture, then in cornmeal mixture. Follow frying procedure as above.*

*For lighter cuisine, pan fry in 1 tablespoon vegetable oil in a non-stick pan or oven-fry at 450°, drizzling catfish with 1 tablespoon vegetable oil.

Makes 4 servings.

Celia Hyde Manse

■ *Old Florida Paella* ■

Beginning with Sally McDowall, four generations of Floridians have tasted and refined this family secret. Practice—in cooking and tasting—has made it perfect!

¼ cup olive oil
¼ cup vegetable oil
1 clove of garlic, slivered
4 large boneless chicken breasts
4 large chicken thighs
1 small green pepper, diced
1 medium onion, diced
1 teaspoon paprika
1 15-ounce can tomatoes
  (chopped) and juice
2½ cups water
1 8-ounce package Dixie Lily
  yellow rice
2 teaspoons salt
1 4-ounce can whole pimientos,
  drained and juice reserved
1 slice ham (½-inch thick), diced
1 7-ounce can minced clams
1 pound raw peeled shrimp
2 20-ounce cans tiny green peas

Combine oils in a Dutch oven; brown garlic clove, then remove. Brown chicken breasts and thighs in the oil. Remove chicken (chicken may be skinned at this point.) Sauté green pepper and onion in remaining oil. Stir in paprika and tomatoes. Add water. Bring to a boil; add rice, salt and liquid *only* from pimientos. Cook rice according to directions. When rice is done, add ham, clams, shrimp and 2 chicken breasts. Bring to a boil for 1 minute. Cover and set aside. When ready to serve, dish up the rice on a large flat serving plate. Place remaining chicken pieces, shrimp, ham, etc. on top of rice. Circle the mound with hot cooked peas. Decorate with long cut strips of pimientos. Clam shells can also be placed on top for decoration. This dish can be prepared in the morning and just heated and served when ready to eat.

Makes 8 to 10 servings.

Amy Blake

• *Easy Florida Baked Grouper* •

This recipe comes from a friend of a friend of a friend, which means each of us has loved this enough to share it with all our friends!

Juice of 2 lemons
4 teaspoons Worcestershire sauce
4 8- to 10-ounce grouper fillets
1 stick butter, melted
  Salt and pepper to taste
2 cups dried bread crumbs
12 Ritz Crackers per fillet, crushed
4 ounces toasted slivered almonds

Mix lemon juice and Worcestershire sauce. Pour over fillets. Marinate for 2 hours. Preheat oven to 400°. Dip fillets in melted butter. Sprinkle with salt and pepper. Combine bread crumbs and crackers. Dredge fillets in crumbs. Place on baking sheet. Bake for 15 minutes at 400°, then lower heat to 300° and bake for 10 minutes. Garnish with slivered almonds. May substitute snapper or any fish that fillets easily.
Makes 4 servings.

Pat Fanning Pirkle

• *Florentine Lasagne Roll-Ups* •

12 fluted lasagne noodles
¾ cup chopped onion
2 tablespoons butter
2 10-ounce packages frozen
  chopped spinach, thawed and
  well drained
1½ cups shredded Mozzarella
  cheese
½ cup sour cream
1 egg, slightly beaten
½ stick butter
¼ cup all-purpose flour
1½ teaspoons instant chicken
  bouillon
⅛ teaspoon pepper
1 cup milk
½ cup grated Parmesan cheese

Cook noodles according to directions. Cool in large bowl of cold water; set aside. Sauté onion in 2 tablespoons butter until tender. Combine spinach, onion, Mozzarella cheese, sour cream and egg. Melt ½ stick butter in saucepan; stir in flour, bouillon and pepper. Gradually add milk. Boil for 1 minute, stirring constantly until thick. Preheat oven to 350°. Pat noodles dry. Spread ¼ cup spinach mixture over each noodle. Roll up jelly-roll style, starting at short end. Spread small amount of sauce in bottom of buttered 2-quart rectangular baking dish. Place rolls in dish. Cover with remaining sauce and cheese. Bake until hot and bubbly.
Makes 6 to 8 servings.

▪ CASSEROLES ▪

A pinch of humor is a wonderful ingredient to add to festivities and food! Many of the names of these casseroles came about because of the good natured fun surrounding the recipe. For instance, "'Twixt Holidays Turkey" is a good name for the casserole served between the traditional turkey days. It was so named by the wife of a man who loved turkey and complained that he had to wait until Thanksgiving or Christmas to get it. This dish was served any time between the holidays to let him know he was special.

The name of "Busy Day Casserole" gives a good idea of how easy this will be and when to fix it. "My Favorite Squash Casserole" and "The-Best-There-Is Broccoli" attest to someone's clear love of these dishes. A favorite here is "Too Late, Can't Wait Soufflé." Be at the table when it's served or you will miss the whole shebang!

▪ *Too Late, Can't Wait Soufflé* ▪

8 ounces sharp cheddar cheese
10 slices buttered bread, crusts removed
4 eggs
2 cups milk
1 teaspoon salt
½ teaspoon dry mustard

Preheat oven to 350°. Put half the cheese, bread, eggs and milk in blender. (It is not necessary to pre-grate cheese.) Turn on high speed until thoroughly mixed. Empty contents into mixing bowl. Repeat with remainder, adding salt and mustard. Pour into mixing bowl. Stir well to combine. Bake in a greased, uncovered 1½-quart casserole for 1 hour. Serve immediately!

Makes 6 to 8 servings.

■ *Spaghetti Casserole* ■

1½ pounds lean ground beef
1 cup chopped onion
1 to 2 cloves garlic, minced
1 28-ounce can tomatoes (home
    canned, if possible)
1 5-ounce can tomato sauce
1 4-ounce can mushrooms,
    drained
2 teaspoons dried oregano
1 teaspoon salt
1 8-ounce package spaghetti,
    cooked and drained
1½ cups grated Mozzarella cheese
⅓ cup grated Parmesan cheese

Brown beef, onion and garlic in Dutch oven. Drain excess fat. Add next 5 ingredients to meat mixture. Simmer gently, uncovered, for 20 to 25 minutes. Preheat oven to 325°. Add spaghetti to meat sauce; pour half the mixture into a greased casserole dish; top with half the combined cheeses. Repeat layers. Bake until bubbly and lightly browned. *Note:* This freezes well.

    Makes 2 medium casseroles or 1 big casserole.

                                Betty Robertson

■ *Busy Day Casserole* ■

This is good alone or with chicken, meatballs or sirloin tips. It is a good side dish for parties, just increase for number of guests. They will love it!

1 cup cooked rice
2 eggs, beaten
½ cup vegetable oil
8 ounces sharp cheddar cheese,
    grated
½ cup minced fresh parsley
1 small onion, chopped
1 clove garlic, pressed
1 small can chopped green chilies
    (juice and all)
1 13-ounce can evaporated milk
    Salt and pepper to taste

Preheat oven to 300°. Combine cooked rice with remaining ingredients. Butter a baking dish and fill with rice mixture. Set dish in a pan containing about 1 inch of water. Bake for 1½ hours or until set.

    Makes 6 servings.

■ *The-Best-There-Is Broccoli Casserole* ■

1 bunch fresh broccoli, cut into
    bite-size pieces
2 eggs, beaten
1 10½-ounce can cheddar cheese
    soup
½ teaspoon oregano
1 16-ounce can stewed tomatoes,
    drained
3 tablespoons Parmesan cheese

Steam fresh broccoli in lightly salted water just until done. Preheat oven to 350°. Combine eggs, soup and oregano and mix well; stir in broccoli and tomatoes. Pour into a lightly greased 1-quart baking dish; sprinkle Parmesan cheese over top. Bake, uncovered, for 30 minutes. *Note:* An optional topping is Italian seasoned bread crumbs; then add the Parmesan cheese.

    Makes 6 to 8 servings.

                           Dorothy Overstreet

Band competitions are big in this part of the world and Moore County High School plays host to the Heart of Tennessee Marching Band Competition each year. Moore County's Band of Spirit is an award winning band—a wonderful reason for every household in the county to celebrate.

▪ *Zucchini-Beef Casserole* ▪

1 pound lean ground chuck
1 8-ounce can tomato sauce
1 teaspoon salt
½ teaspoon sugar
1 teaspoon Worcestershire sauce
¼ teaspoon hot pepper sauce
2 green onions, finely chopped
1 pound zucchini, thinly sliced
1 3-ounce package cream cheese, softened
1 8-ounce carton sour cream
2 tablespoons seasoned dry bread crumbs or grated Parmesan cheese
Paprika

Preheat oven to 350°. Brown meat in large skillet over medium heat, stirring to crumble. Add tomato sauce, salt, sugar, Worcestershire sauce and hot pepper sauce. Cook over medium heat for 5 minutes, stirring occasionally. Remove from heat; stir in green onions. Spoon half the meat mixture into a greased 10x6x2-inch baking dish. Top with half the zucchini slices. Repeat layers. Combine cream cheese and sour cream; spread evenly over casserole. Sprinkle with bread crumbs or Parmesan cheese, then paprika. Bake for 35 minutes.
Makes 6 servings.

June Tucker

▪ *Zucchini Seafood Casserole* ▪

4 cups zucchini, unpeeled and uncooked, sliced ¼-inch thick
½ cup vegetable oil
1½ cups cubed sharp cheese
1½ cups Bisquick
1 10-ounce can crabmeat or albacore tuna, drained
3 eggs, slightly beaten
1 cup chopped onion
1 teaspoon oregano
1 teaspoon salt
½ teaspoon pepper

Preheat oven to 400°. Combine all ingredients; mix well. Pour into a greased 12x7x2-inch baking dish. Bake, uncovered, for 30 minutes.
Makes 6 servings.

Artie M. Renegar

79

About once in every century a really special celebration takes place. The introduction of Gentleman Jack, the first new whiskey from the Jack Daniel Distillery in one hundred years, was just such an event. The Moore County High School Band played, the press and media covered the event, and hundreds of balloons filled the air. It was a wonderful celebration!

▪ *Our Favorite Turkey Casserole* ▪

I am always amazed that people look for things to do with leftover turkey. Turkey has been a favorite of our family and there were more dishes to make than we had turkey. Here is a dish that would use what was left on the carcass before it went into the turkey vegetable soup pot.

4 ounces linguini or elbow macaroni
2 teaspoons salt
½ stick butter
¼ cup all-purpose flour
½ teaspoon salt
½ teaspoon pepper
1 cup light cream or half-and-half
1 10¾-ounce can cream of mushroom soup
¾ cup canned peas, drained
1 2-ounce jar chopped pimientos, drained
1 cup chopped cooked turkey
1 cup shredded cheddar or Velveeta cheese

Preheat oven to 350°. Cook linguini in 3 cups boiling water with 2 teaspoons salt. Stir and boil rapidly for 2 minutes. Cover and remove from heat; let stand 10 minutes. Melt butter in saucepan; stir in flour, salt and pepper. Add cream gradually to keep from lumping; blend in soup. Cook until thickened, stirring constantly. Drain linguini and rinse with warm water; drain well. Add sauce, peas, pimiento and turkey to linguini, turning gently to blend. Pour into a greased-2 quart casserole and top with shredded cheese. Bake for 20 minutes or until cheese is melted and bubbly.

Makes 6 to 8 servings.

■ 'Twixt Holidays Turkey ■

1 cup celery, chopped
1 onion, chopped
Butter
1 pound processed American
cheese, cubed
¼ cup milk
0 cups diced cooked turkey
1 2-ounce jar pimientos, chopped
and drained
1 16-ounce can French-style green
beans, drained
2 cups noodles, cooked and
drained
¼ cup crushed crackers

Preheat oven to 350°. Sauté celery and onion in 1 tablespoon butter. Add half the cubed cheese and milk to celery mixture. Stir over low heat until the sauce is smooth. Add turkey, pimiento and green beans, stir to mix. Layer noodles in a greased 10x6x2-inch baking dish; top with turkey mixture. Cover turkey with crushed crackers; dot with butter. Bake for 25 minutes. Remove from oven and top with remaining cheese. Return to oven; bake just until cheese melts.

Makes 6 to 8 servings.

Vivian Mitchamore

■ Baked Chicken Salad ■

2 cups chopped cooked chicken
1½ cups chopped almonds
½ cup mayonnaise
1 10¾-ounce can cream of chicken
soup, undiluted
2 cups chopped celery
2 tablespoons grated onion
2 tablespoons chopped pimiento
½ teaspoon salt
2 tablespoons lemon juice
½ cup chopped green pepper
½ cup grated American cheese
3 cups crushed potato chips

Preheat oven to 350°. Combine all ingredients, except cheese and chips. Toss lightly and pour into a greased 1½-quart casserole dish. Top with cheese and chips. Bake for 25 to 30 minutes or until hot and bubbly.

Makes 8 servings.

Wildred Patton

■ Asparagus And Chicken Casserole ■

2 cups chopped cooked chicken
1 15-ounce can drained tiny green
peas
2 10½-ounce cans cream of
chicken soup
2 cans of half-and-half, measured
in soup can
2 cups elbow macaroni, uncooked
1 15-ounce can asparagus spears,
drained
1 cup grated sharp cheddar cheese

Preheat oven to 350°. Combine chicken, peas, soup, half-and-half and uncooked elbow macaroni in a greased 3-quart casserole. Arrange asparagus spears on top; cover with cheese. Bake, covered, for 1 hour, uncover the last 15 minutes.

Makes 6 to 8 servings.

Marian Baird

81

▪ *Yum Chicken Casserole* ▪

Ritz Crackers or other butter
cracker
1 stick butter
1 whole chicken, cooked in water
until tender, deboned and meat
cut into bite-size pieces
1 cup chopped celery
1 cup cooked rice
2 tablespoons minced onion
1 10¾-ounce can cream of
mushroom soup
⅔ cup salad dressing
¾ teaspoon salt
¼ teaspoon pepper

Preheat oven to 350°. Crumble crackers. Melt butter in saucepan; stir in cracker crumbs and set aside. Mix remaining ingredients; place in a greased 13x9x2-inch baking dish. Top with cracker crumb mixture. Bake for about 30 minutes or until browned and bubbly.
Makes 6 servings.

Thelma Grisham

▪ *Quick Chick Trick* ▪

This is one of those real easy—but also real good—recipes.

4 chicken breasts
1 cup sour cream
1 10½-ounce can cream of chicken
soup
40 Ritz crackers, crumbled
1 stick butter

Preheat oven to 350°. Boil and debone chicken. Cut into bite-size pieces and place in bottom of greased baking dish. Mix sour cream and soup in saucepan and heat. Pour over chicken pieces. Crumble crackers over mixture. Melt butter and pour over crackers. Bake for 20 minutes.
Makes 4 servings.

Verna Steelman

▪ *Classic Ham Casserole* ▪

2 tablespoons butter or margarine
1 cup finely chopped onion
3 cups ground cooked ham
1 10-ounce package frozen
chopped broccoli, thawed
12 slices wheat or white bread
Butter or margarine, softened
3 cups grated sharp cheddar
cheese
6 eggs, beaten
3½ cups milk
¾ teaspoon dry mustard
½ teaspoon salt

Melt 2 tablespoons butter in skillet; sauté onion until tender. In medium bowl, combine onion, ham and broccoli. Trim crusts from bread. Butter bread; set aside. Arrange 6 bread slices on bottom of buttered 13x9x2-inch casserole. Top with ham mixture; then with cheese. Place remaining bread slices on top of cheese. Combine eggs, milk, mustard and salt; pour over bread slices. Cover; chill for 6 hours or overnight. When ready to bake, preheat oven to 325°. Bake, uncovered, for 1 hour. Let set a few minutes before serving.
Makes 8 to 10 servings.

Andy Rambo

▪ *Squash Casserole* ▪

¼ cup green pepper, chopped
¼ cup onion, chopped
2 tablespoons butter
2 cups yellow squash, cut into
   pieces, cooked and well drained
¼ cup chopped pimiento
1 10¾-ounce can cream of
   mushroom soup
½ cup processed cheese, grated
1 teaspoon salt
   Black pepper to taste
1 cup seasoned bread crumbs

Preheat oven to 350°. Sauté pepper and onion in butter. Combine with squash, pimiento, soup, cheese, salt and pepper. Place mixture in greased casserole dish. Top with bread crumbs. Bake for 30 minutes or until bubbly. Makes 6 servings.

Barbara Ruth McGowan

▪ *Favorite Squash Casserole* ▪

5 large yellow summer squash,
   chopped
1 large onion, chopped
   Salt and pepper
2 eggs
1 cup cracker crumbs
½ stick butter, softened
6 slices American cheese

Combine squash and onion in saucepan; cover with water. Add salt and pepper to taste. Cook until tender; remove from heat and drain. Preheat oven to 350°. Place squash mixture in a large greased casserole dish and mash with a fork. Beat eggs; mix into squash. Blend in crumbs, butter and 4 slices of cheese. Use remaining cheese to top casserole. Bake for 45 minutes.
   Makes 8 servings.

Patty Ayers

▪ *My Sweet Potato Soufflé* ▪

My favorite sweet potato recipe.

2 cups mashed cooked sweet
   potatoes
¾ stick butter, softened
1¼ cups sugar
½ teaspoon nutmeg
½ teaspoon cinnamon
2 beaten eggs
1 cup evaporated milk
½ stick butter
¾ cup crushed cornflakes
½ cup packed brown sugar
½ cup pecan pieces

Preheat oven to 350°. Combine first 7 ingredients. Pour into buttered casserole dish. Bake for 20 minutes. While soufflé is baking, melt butter; stir in cornflakes, brown sugar and nuts. Spread over top of soufflé. Bake 10 minutes longer or until set. *Note:* If canned potatoes are used, use only ½ cup milk.
   Makes 4 to 6 servings.

Wilma Bedford

83

• *Hominy Casserole* •

½ stick butter
¼ cup all-purpose flour
1 teaspoon onion powder
2 cups milk, heated
1 cup grated processed cheese
1 29-ounce can hominy, drained
1 cup Ritz cracker crumbs,
   buttered

Preheat oven to 350°. Melt the butter over low heat; blend in flour and onion powder. Slowly stir in the heated milk. Stir the sauce with a wire whisk or wooden spoon over low heat until thickened and smooth. Stir in cheese until melted; add the hominy. Pour into a greased casserole dish; top with buttered cracker crumbs. Bake for 30 minutes or until hot and bubbly.
   Makes 6 servings.

Velma Waggoner

• *Mixed Squash Casserole* •

3 cups sliced yellow squash
3 cups sliced zucchini squash
2 tablespoons chopped onion
3 tablespoons butter or margarine
1½ teaspoons chopped fresh parsley
¼ teaspoon dried basil
1½ cups shredded cheddar cheese,
   divided
1 cup cracker crumbs, divided

Preheat oven to 350°. Cook squash in water until tender; drain and mash. Combine onion, butter, parsley, basil, half the cheese and half the crumbs. Pour into greased casserole dish; top with remaining crumbs and cheese. Bake for 30 to 45 minutes until bubbly and beginning to brown.
   Makes 6 to 8 servings.

Wilma Bedford

• *Crouton Brunch Casserole* •

This Crouton Brunch Casserole is very easy to make and a little different using croutons for bread. It is an excellent brunch dish!

2¼ cups seasoned croutons
1½ pounds bulk pork sausage
4 eggs, beaten
2¼ cups milk
1 10¾-ounce can cream of
   mushroom soup, undiluted
1 4-ounce can sliced mushrooms,
   drained
¾ teaspoon dry mustard
2 cups (8 ounces) shredded
   cheddar cheese
   Cherry tomato halves, optional
   Parsley sprigs, optional

Spread croutons in a lightly greased 13x9x2-inch baking dish; set aside. Cook sausage until browned, stirring to crumble; drain well. Sprinkle sausage over croutons. Combine eggs, milk, soup, mushrooms and mustard; mix well and pour over sausage. Cover and chill at least 8 hours or overnight. Remove from refrigerator; let stand 30 minutes. Preheat oven to 325°. Bake, uncovered, for 50 to 55 minutes. Sprinkle cheese over top; bake an additional 5 minutes or until cheese melts. Garnish with tomatoes and parsley, if desired.
   Makes 8 servings.

Florence McKeithan

84

Ladies of Lynchburg Handicraft Shop

Beautiful handmade quilts, country sunbonnets, and crocheted and knitted afghans, sweaters, and baby sets are among the many items for sale at the Ladies of Lynchburg Handicraft Shop on the Square. Some years ago a number of ladies from the area got together to discuss a way to market their varied and beautiful handmade items. The handicraft shop was born from this meeting.

To display and sell their items, each lady contributes a day of her time each month. While at the shop she might pick up a needle and help a friend finish a quilt or she might dust the shelves or sweep the floor. Each person gives generously to help make the store a success and a place where visitors will enjoy coming. Over the years, many visitors have bought lovingly created gifts.

When you are in Lynchburg, stop in and visit with the ladies. Your visit is something special to them, and they want you to feel at home. Browse through the shop to see if you can find the perfect gift for Aunt Dorothy, sister Doris, or cousin Susie. A bonnet for Sabrina, an Easter dress for Amber, or a christening dress for Ryan may be found in this collection of beautiful homemade items. Or take home a gift for yourself to remember the occasion of your trip to Lynchburg.

▪ *Curried Sausage Casserole* ▪

2 pounds bulk pork sausage, browned, crumbled and well drained
2 small green peppers, diced
¼ pound sliced mushrooms
2 tablespoons margarine
2 tablespoons all-purpose flour
1 teaspoon curry powder
1½ cups milk
1 cup bread crumbs
   Parmesan cheese

Preheat oven to 350°. Combine all ingredients, except bread crumbs and Parmesan cheese; place in greased baking dish. Cover with bread crumbs and a sprinkling of Parmesan cheese. Bake for 30 minutes.
   Makes 8 servings.

Verna Steelman

▪ *Cheesy Egg Casserole* ▪

¼ cup all-purpose flour
¼ teaspoon salt
½ stick margarine, melted
4 eggs, beaten
1 cup cottage cheese
1 2-ounce can chopped green chilies, drained
2 cups Monterey jack cheese, shredded
1 4-ounce jar pimientos, drained
   Green pepper rings

Preheat oven to 375°. Combine flour, salt and margarine in a large bowl. Add eggs, cottage cheese, green chilies and cheese. Mix well. Pour mixture into a lightly greased 10x6x2-inch baking dish. Garnish with pimientos and green pepper rings. Bake, uncovered, for 30 minutes.
   Makes 6 servings.

Verna Steelman

▪ *Hash-Brown Potato Casserole* ▪

1 32-ounce package frozen hash-brown potatoes, thawed
1 16-ounce carton sour cream
2 cups grated sharp cheddar cheese
1 stick butter or margarine, melted
1 10¾-ounce can cream of mushroom soup
½ cup finely chopped onion
   Buttered cracker crumbs

Preheat oven to 350°. Combine all ingredients, except cracker crumbs. Pour into a greased casserole. Top with buttered cracker crumbs. Bake for 1 hour.
   Makes 8 servings.

Kathleen Fanning

■ *Church Supper Casserole* ■

This is a wonderful church supper casserole. Easy to fix, easy to take, liked by everyone . . . and pretty, too!

1 pound bulk pork sausage, browned, crumbled and well drained
1 cup quick-cooking rice
1 onion, chopped
1 10½-ounce can cream of chicken soup
1 10¾-ounce can cream of mushroom soup
1 2-ounce jar pimientos, drained and chopped
1 cup sharp cheddar cheese, grated (reserve ¼ cup for topping)

Preheat oven to 300°. Combine all ingredients, except the reserved cheese. Place in a lightly buttered casserole dish. Cover top with reserved cheese. Bake for approximately 1 hour or until hot and bubbly and lightly browned on top.

Makes 6 servings.

Mrs. Lilbern Rutledge

Part of the fun of a hometown fair is looking for an unexpected treasure. It might be a new item created by an artisan who is continuing the traditions of the past or it might be an antique that is just like something you remember from your grandparents' home. In Lynchburg booths on the courthouse square, concessions, and food stands are all part of the fun too.

87

▪ VEGETABLES ▪

I t is surprising to discover how many different ways vegetables are used to add to the bounty of our tables. Combined with a variety of ingredients, they can achieve many different tastes, and become different dishes. Good cooks look to the garden to produce a wide range of vegetables and grains that stretch food dollars and provide a wealth of tasty, healthy dishes. Vegetables and side dishes add variety and excitement to everyday meals. Here is a collection of outstanding recipes.

▪ *Baked Apples and Cheese* ▪

This travels well to dinner on the grounds, family reunions, and picnics. It is wonderful as a side dish to pork. Serve hot or cold. It is my most asked for recipe!

2 cups sliced peeled apples
¾ cup sugar
¾ cup all-purpose flour
1 stick butter or margarine, melted
½ pound diced Velveeta processed
   cheese

Preheat oven to 350°. Place apples in buttered casserole. Combine sugar, flour, butter and cheese. Spread over apples; stir just enough to spread mixture throughout apples. Bake for 40 minutes or until bubbly in center and brownish on top.

Makes 6 servings.

Sue Upchurch

In Lynchburg, toes tap to the typical sounds of Tennessee's hills and hollows. Here a special group of men plays bluegrass music with stringed instruments and performs for many of the events in town. Since they all work for the Jack Daniel Distillery, they call themselves the Barrel House Gang.

■ *Candied Apples* ■

6 cups apples, chopped
4 cups sugar
1 stick butter
1 tablespoon cinnamon

Preheat oven to 375°. Place all ingredients in a saucepan and cook, stirring occasionally until butter melts and sugar is dissolved. Pour the mixture into a greased 9x9-inch baking dish. Bake for 40 minutes or until apples are tender and sauce is bubbly.

Makes 8 to 10 servings.

Served at Miss Mary Bobo's Boarding House

■ *Asparagus Casserole* ■

1 cup sharp cheddar cheese, grated
2 cups saltine crackers, crumbled
3 tablespoons butter
1 10¾-ounce can cream of mushroom soup
1 14½-ounce can asparagus, drained and juice reserved
⅓ cup slivered almonds

Preheat oven to 350°. Mix grated cheese and crumbled crackers; set aside. Heat butter, soup and reserved asparagus juice. In a greased casserole dish, layer half the crumb mixture, asparagus and almonds; cover with half the soup mixture. Repeat layers ending with crumbs. Bake for about 20 minutes until hot and bubbly.

Makes 6 servings.

Bonnie Darnell

90

• *Harvard Beets* •

1¾ cups vinegar, divided
1 teaspoon salt
1½ cups sugar
3 tablespoons cornstarch
2 teaspoons allspice
3 cups beets

Place 1½ cups vinegar, salt and sugar in a saucepan. Bring to a boil. Mix cornstarch and allspice together; add ¼ cup vinegar. Add to hot liquid. Stir well and cook until thickened. Add beets. Heat and serve.
Makes 6 to 8 servings.

Served at Miss Mary Bobo's Boarding House

• *Broccoli Italienne* •

This makes an attractive dish. Serve it with Thanksgiving or Christmas dinner.

2 1-pound bunches fresh broccoli
2 cups water
½ teaspoon dried whole oregano
½ teaspoon salt
½ cup mayonnaise
¼ cup shredded cheddar cheese
1 tablespoon milk

Trim off large leaves of broccoli; remove tough ends of lower stalks. Wash broccoli thoroughly; separate into spears. Combine water, oregano and salt in a large saucepan; bring to a boil and add broccoli. Cover; reduce heat and simmer for 8 to 10 minutes or until tender. Drain well; arrange on serving dish. Combine mayonnaise, cheese and milk in a small saucepan; cover over low heat until cheese melts, stirring constantly. Spoon mixture over broccoli.
Makes 8 servings.

Wilma Bedford

• *Scalloped Corn* •

42 saltine crackers, crumbled
3 16½-ounce cans cream-style corn
1½ tablespoons dehydrated onion flakes
½ teaspoon dry mustard
¼ cup chopped green and red peppers
¼ teaspoon pepper
Butter
Paprika

Preheat oven to 350°. Combine all ingredients, except butter and paprika; mix well. Pour into a lightly greased 2-quart casserole dish. Dot with butter; sprinkle top with paprika. Bake for 50 minutes or until the top is bubbling and golden brown. Remove from oven; let stand for 10 minutes to set.
Makes 8 servings.

Velma Ray

91

▪ *Spicy Corn* ▪

2 12-ounce cans shoe-peg corn
1 8-ounce package cream cheese
1 stick butter
¼ cup milk
½ teaspoon seasoned salt
¼ cup chopped green chili peppers
    Tortilla chips

Preheat oven to 350°. Drain corn; set aside. In saucepan over low heat, combine cream cheese, butter, milk and seasoned salt. Heat slowly, stirring to prevent sticking. Add corn and peppers. Pour into a buttered baking dish; top with crushed tortilla chips. Bake for 30 minutes. Serve hot.
    Makes 6 to 8 servings.

▪ *Aunt Christine's Cucumber Casserole* ▪

Several summers ago my husband and I and a large group from Sewanee enjoyed a delightful dinner at Miss Bobo's. They mentioned that they wanted some new ideas for cucumbers. I said I had a good casserole with cucumbers and I'd send the recipe. Here it is!

4 cucumbers, peeled, sliced and
    boiled until tender
    Sliced water chestnuts to taste
1 cup homemade white sauce
¼ cup mayonnaise
    Salt and pepper to taste
    Bread crumbs
    Paprika
    Butter

Preheat oven to 325°. Place a layer of cucumbers and a layer of water chestnuts in a greased casserole. Combine white sauce, mayonnaise, salt and pepper. Spread half the sauce over cucumber mixture. Repeat layers. Top with bread crumbs, paprika and dots of butter. Bake for 20 minutes or until bubbly throughout.
Makes 4 to 6 servings.

Amelia Montjoy

▪ *Eggplant Parmesan* ▪

¼ cup Parmesan cheese
½ cup cornmeal
2 to 3 small eggplants, peeled and
    cut into ½-inch slices
1 stick margarine, melted
1 8-ounce can pizza sauce
1 4-ounce package grated
    Mozzarella cheese

Preheat oven to 400°. Mix Parmesan cheese and cornmeal. Dip eggplant in melted margarine. Roll in cornmeal mixture. Place in greased pan. Cover with pizza sauce; top with Mozzarella. Bake for 15 to 20 minutes.
    Makes 6 servings.

Chris Baker

▪ *Company Green Beans* ▪

1 16-ounce can French-style green
beans, drained
1 16-ounce can bean sprouts,
drained
1 8-ounce can sliced water
chestnuts, drained
1 10¾-ounce can cream of
mushroom soup
1 small onion, finely chopped
1 cup grated cheddar cheese

Preheat oven to 350°. Combine first 5 ingredients in greased 3-quart casserole. Blend in ⅔ cup cheese. Sprinkle remaining cheese on top. Bake for 30 to 40 minutes.

Makes 12 servings.

▪ *Grits Casserole* ▪

4 cups water
1 teaspoon garlic powder or more
1 teaspoon salt
¼ teaspoon pepper
1 cup quick-cooking grits
2 tablespoons butter or margarine
1½ cups grated processed cheese,
divided
2 eggs, beaten
½ cup milk

Preheat oven to 350°. In a large saucepan, bring the water to a boil. Add garlic powder, salt and pepper. Gradually stir in grits. Lower heat and simmer, stirring occasionally for 5 minutes. Remove pan from heat, stir in butter and 1 cup cheese until melted. Mix eggs with milk; stir into grits. Pour grits into a greased 2-quart casserole. Sprinkle with remaining cheese. Bake for 1 hour.

Makes 4 to 6 servings.

Served at Miss Mary Bobo's Boarding House

Parades in Lynchburg are big events. At Christmas Santa comes to town riding on a fire engine. There is a tree lighting at the Gazebo Park and the children's choir sings as the Christmas lights are turned on. The parade doesn't rival Macy's Thanksgiving Day Parade in New York City, but it is the biggest one in Lynchburg each year.

• *Hopping John* •

According to legend, Hopping John is the dish that began the whole peas-and-luck superstition.

"A dish known as hoppinjohn, which consists of black-eyed peas cooked with hog jowl, is the traditional New Year's dinner in many families. This custom began in Civil War days; some planters who had nothing to eat but black-eyed peas at New Year's dinner were lucky enough to regain their fortunes, and later on they somehow connected this good luck with the New Year's hoppinjohn," states Vance Randolph in his book Ozark Magic and Folklore.

1 cup dried black-eyed peas
8 cups water
6 slices bacon
¾ cup chopped onion
1 clove garlic, minced
1 cup regular rice, uncooked
2 teaspoons salt
¼ teaspoon pepper
  Onions
  Cornbread

Rinse the black-eyed peas. In a large saucepan, combine the peas and water. Bring to a boil; boil for 2 minutes. Remove from heat; set aside for 1 hour. Drain, reserving 6 cups of the cooking liquid. In a heavy 3-quart stew pan, cook the bacon, onion and garlic until bacon is crisp and onion is tender, but not brown. Remove bacon; drain on paper towels; crumble and set aside. Stir the black-eyed peas, raw rice, salt, pepper and the reserved cooking liquid into onion mixture in stew pan. Bring to a boil; cover and reduce heat. Simmer for 1 hour, stirring occasionally. Stir in crumbled bacon. Serve immediately with sliced onions and cornbread.

Makes 8 servings.

Norma Rigler

• *Macaroni and Cheese* •

8 cups water
2 teaspoons salt
¼ cup vegetable oil
2 cups macaroni
2½ cups grated processed cheese, divided
½ stick butter

Preheat oven to 350°. Bring water and salt to a boil. Add oil and macaroni, stirring occasionally. Cook until tender; drain. Add 2 cups grated cheese and butter. Pour mixture into a greased 9x13-inch baking dish. Top with remaining cheese. Bake for 30 minutes or until hot and bubbly.

Makes 6 to 8 servings.

Served at Miss Mary Bobo's Boarding House

• *Fried Okra* •

1 10-ounce box frozen sliced okra,
  thawed, or 1½ cups sliced fresh
  okra, blanched and cooled
1 cup cornmeal
½ cup all-purpose flour
⅛ teaspoon salt
  Vegetable oil

Place okra in a bowl. Mix cornmeal, flour and salt. Coat okra pieces with mixture. Let stand for at least an hour. (This keeps the coating from falling off during the frying). Heat ½-inch deep oil in a heavy skillet. When oil is hot, add okra one layer deep (do not crowd skillet). Cook until browned on one side, about 5 minutes, then turn and cook on the other side. Drain on paper towels. Can also be fried in deep-fat fryer.

Makes 6 servings.

Velma Jean Waggoner

• *Glazed Onions* •

1 pound pearl onions, peeled
2 tablespoons butter or margarine
1 tablespoon brown sugar
½ teaspoon cornstarch
¼ teaspoon salt
¼ teaspoon dry mustard
  Dash of pepper
1 tablespoon cider vinegar

Combine onions and butter in a 1½-quart casserole. Cover and microwave on HIGH for 6 to 8 minutes, or until tender, stirring once. Drain; reserve liquid. In a small bowl, combine brown sugar, cornstarch and seasonings. Stir in vinegar and reserved cooking liquid. Microwave on HIGH for 45 to 60 seconds, or until clear and thickened. Pour sauce over onions. Toss to coat.

Makes 4 to 6 servings.

Mary Kathryn Holt

• *English Pea Casserole* •

This recipe was given to me in 1970 by Nell Fanning. It is really good.

1 onion, chopped
½ green pepper, chopped
4 ribs celery, chopped fine
1 stick margarine
1 4-ounce can mushrooms,
  chopped and drained
1 10¾-ounce can cream of
  mushroom soup
1 2-ounce jar pimientos, chopped
  and drained, reserve liquid
2 17-ounce cans English peas,
  drained, reserve liquid
  Bread crumbs
  Margarine

Preheat oven to 350°. Sauté onion, pepper and celery in margarine. Mix mushrooms, soup and 1 cup reserved pea liquid and pimiento. Combine all ingredients in a large greased casserole dish; top with bread crumbs and dot with margarine. Bake for 30 minutes or until hot and bubbly.

Makes 6 servings.

Ruth Daniel

95

• *Escalloped Pineapple* •

3 eggs
1 cup sugar
1 stick margarine, melted
1 large can crushed pineapple, drained
1 quart bread crumbs

Preheat oven to 350°. Beat eggs; stir in sugar and margarine. Add pineapple and bread crumbs; mix well until all bread crumbs are well soaked. Pour into a greased baking dish. Bake for 45 minutes until hot and golden brown. Delicious!
Makes 6 to 8 servings.

Martha Burrus

• *Church Supper Potatoes* •

1½ pounds potatoes, peeled, cubed and cooked
1 bunch green onions, chopped
1 cup Mozzarella cheese, shredded
1 cup sharp cheddar cheese, shredded
1 teaspoon celery seed
12 large eggs
1½ cups sour cream
1 quart half-and-half
Salt and pepper to taste
Paprika

Preheat oven to 325°. Combine potatoes, onion, cheeses and celery seed; set aside. Beat eggs with electric mixer on low speed. Add sour cream, half-and-half, salt and pepper. Stir into the potato mixture until blended. Pour into a greased 10x12x2-inch baking dish or use 2 loaf pans. Sprinkle top with paprika. Bake, uncovered, for 30 minutes. Cover; bake 30 minutes longer. Let stand for 15 minutes. Slice into portions and serve.
Makes 12 servings.

• *Scalloped Rhubarb* •

3 tablespoons butter
2 cups soft bread crumbs
1½ cups sugar
¼ teaspoon cinnamon
Dash of nutmeg
3 cups rhubarb, cut into 1-inch pieces
⅓ cup water

Preheat oven to 350°. Melt butter; stir in bread crumbs and set aside. Mix sugar and spices. Butter a 1½-quart baking dish; cover bottom with ¼ the crumb mixture. Top with half of the rhubarb and half of the sugar mixture. Repeat layers. Pour water gently over all. Top with remaining crumbs. Bake for 1½ hours, rhubarb should be thoroughly cooked. Cover and cool for at least 1 hour before serving.
Makes 6 servings.

▪ *Green Rice* ▪

This dish is delicious with almost anything, but a lot of folks think it is especially good with Mexican food instead of Spanish rice.

1 cup rice, uncooked
1 cup sour cream
1 8-ounce can chopped green
   chilies
   Salt and pepper to taste
½ pound Monterey jack cheese,
   shredded
   Butter

Preheat oven to 350°. Cook rice according to package directions. Mix cooked rice, sour cream, green chilies and seasonings. Place half the mixture in a greased baking dish. Top with a layer of shredded cheese. Repeat layers; top with dots of butter. Bake for 30 minutes or until heated throughout.
   Makes 4 to 6 servings.

Dorothy Overstreet

▪ *Quick And Easy Spinach Delight* ▪

2 cups ricotta cheese
4 10-ounce packages frozen
   chopped spinach, cooked and
   well drained
10 slices Muenster cheese

Preheat oven to 350°. Mix ricotta with spinach. Line bottom of greased casserole dish with half the Muenster cheese. Spread spinach mixture over top; cover with the remaining cheese. Bake for 25 minutes or until top is bubbling and golden brown. Remove from oven; let stand for approximately 20 minutes to allow the cheese to set. Using a spatula, cut into squares and serve.
   Makes 8 servings.

Dusty Sue Hellerman

▪ *Spana Kopita* ▪

3 eggs
6 tablespoons all-purpose flour
2 cups cottage cheese
1 teaspoon salt
1 10-ounce package frozen
   chopped spinach, thawed and
   drained
1 cup shredded cheddar cheese
1 4-ounce can chopped
   mushrooms, drained
   Cracked pepper to taste

Preheat oven to 350°. Beat eggs with flour until smooth; stir in cottage cheese and salt. Fold in spinach, cheese, mushrooms and pepper. Place in a greased 2-quart casserole dish. Bake for 1 hour until hot and bubbly.
   Makes 6 to 8 servings.

▪ *Dutch Scalloped Spinach* ▪

1 pound fresh spinach
1 egg, beaten
1 cup milk
1 stick butter, melted
½ teaspoon salt
  Pepper to taste
¼ cup chopped, cooked bacon
1 cup toasted bread crumbs,
  divided

Preheat oven to 350°. Cook and chop spinach. Add remaining ingredients, except bacon and ½ cup bread crumbs. Mix well; pour into a greased 1-quart casserole. Sprinkle remaining crumbs and bacon on top. Bake for 35 to 40 minutes.
Makes 4 to 6 servings.

▪ *Spinach-Stuffed Shells* ▪

3 tablespoons cornstarch
1 teaspoon salt
3 cups milk
½ stick margarine
1½ cups grated Swiss cheese
½ cup chopped onion
1 cup chopped fresh mushrooms
2 tablespoons vegetable oil
⅛ teaspoon pepper
  Salt to taste
1 10-ounce package frozen
  spinach, thawed and drained
1 pound ricotta cheese or dry
  cottage cheese
1 package jumbo pasta shells,
  cooked and drained
⅓ cup Parmesan cheese

In a 2-quart saucepan, mix cornstarch and salt. Gradually stir in milk until smooth; add margarine. Stirring constantly, bring to a boil over medium heat; boil for 1 minute. Stir in Swiss cheese. Blend well; remove from heat and set aside. Preheat oven to 350°. Sauté onion and mushrooms in oil until tender. Season with pepper and salt. Mix spinach and ricotta cheese into mushroom mixture. Stuff pasta shells with filling and place in a 10x13-inch greased baking dish. Pour cheese sauce over stuffed shells and sprinkle with Parmesan cheese. Bake for 20 to 25 minutes or until bubbling and lightly browned.
Makes 8 servings.

Melody Ray

▪ *Squash Croquettes* ▪

2 cups raw squash
1 cup onion
1 cup water
1 egg, beaten
8 tablespoons (or more) all-
  purpose flour
1 teaspoon salt
2 teaspoons pepper
  Vegetable oil

Combine squash, onion and water in blender; chop and drain well. Stir in egg. Add enough flour to make batter the consistency of batter for hush puppies. Blend in salt and pepper. Drop by heaping tablespoonsful into hot oil. Drain on paper towels. Serve hot.
Makes 8 servings.

Rada Manley

Easter and Family Celebrations

Rada Manley and Marsha Russell

Annual family celebrations are the core of all of our other celebrations. There is something about certain holidays that says "home" and "family." Also, at the core of our communities are certain families headed by a person who is revered and respected. Such a person was Charles Manley, who for many years was executive vice president of the Jack Daniel Distillery. He was the head of a unique family in Lynchburg of company employees. Lynchburg is a company town, and his untimely death was a great loss to his friends and family.

Charles' son, Charlie, Jr., and his daughter, Marsha Russell, both work for the distillery. Family get-togethers include their mother, Rada, and their families. Marsha's children, Colt and Corrie, are the youngest of the five grandchildren. Family celebrations are made more special and wonderful because of their presence.

Easter is a family time when we can celebrate the hope and promise of the future. It is also very special to little children because of the colored eggs, the egg hunt, candies, and new clothes. Easter holds a greater meaning for the older generation. Spring follows the dead of winter, reminding us of new life. Spring bursts forth in living brilliant color. It is a time of great celebration. It is Easter that reveals the true gift of Christmas. With flowers, fun, festivities, food, and family, Easter is truly a time to celebrate life.

■ *Sweet Potato Soufflé* ■

3 cups cooked mashed sweet
   potatoes
1 cup sugar
2 eggs
½ cup milk
½ teaspoon salt
1 teaspoon vanilla
1 cup packed brown sugar
½ cup all-purpose flour
1 cup chopped pecans
½ stick butter, room temperature

Preheat oven to 400°. Combine first 6 ingredients; mix well. Pour into buttered pan. Combine remaining ingredients. Spread over sweet potato mixture. Bake for 30 to 40 minutes or until firm in center.
   Makes 4 to 6 servings.

■ *Vi's Famous Baked Tomatoes* ■

3 cups canned tomatoes, drained
   and chopped
1 cup sugar
2 sticks butter
1 tablespoon basil
6 slices white bread, toasted and
   crumbled

Preheat oven to 350°. Place tomatoes, sugar and butter in a saucepan and heat until the butter melts. Add basil and bread crumbs; continue simmering until most of the liquid is absorbed, about 15 minutes. Pour into a greased 9x9-inch baking dish. Bake for about 20 to 30 minutes or until thick.
   Makes 6 servings.
         Served at Miss Mary Bobo's Boarding House

■ *String Beans and Glazed Tomatoes* ■

This is a traditional dish in our family on Christmas and sometimes at Thanksgiving. I never have enough for seconds or thirds! It is very good with roast beef and mashed potatoes. I received it from my mother who always made it for special days.

1 quart tomatoes
¾ cup sugar
¼ cup vinegar
   Cooked string beans

Combine tomatoes, sugar and vinegar in a cast-iron skillet. Bring to a boil. Lower heat; simmer for 1 hour, stirring occasionally. Mix with hot cooked string beans.
   Makes 4 to 6 servings.
         Betty J. Grimm

■ *Pure Delight Turnips* ■

4 medium turnips
3 tablespoons butter
3 tablespoons all-purpose flour
1 cup half and half
1 10½-ounce can cheddar cheese
  soup, undiluted
¼ teaspoon salt
  Crackers, optional

Peel and slice turnips, cover with salted water and cook 15 minutes. Remove from stove and drain. In another saucepan melt butter, stir in flour and gradually add half-and-half. Stir constantly until white sauce is slightly thickened. Add soup and salt; blend well. Preheat oven to 350°. Place turnips in a greased baking dish; pour cheese sauce over. May top with crushed crackers, if desired. Bake for about 25 minutes or until hot and bubbly.
  Makes 4 servings.

■ *Cold Vegetable Medley* ■

1½ cups mayonnaise
2 hard-boiled eggs, finely chopped
1 medium onion, finely chopped
1 tablespoon Worcestershire sauce
1 tablespoon prepared mustard
¼ teaspoon salt
  Juice of 1 lemon
½ teaspoon garlic salt
  Dash of hot pepper sauce
3 cups frozen peas
2 10-ounce packages frozen lima
  beans
2 10-ounce packages frozen
  French-style green beans

Combine first 9 ingredients, stirring well. Chill several hours. When ready to use, bring to room temperature. Cook frozen vegetables according to package directions. Drain. Add sauce, stirring gently to coat. Serve immediately.
  Makes 10 to 12 servings.

Nancye Shannon

101

· DESSERTS ·

"To get your just desserts" means to get what you deserve, but in a negative way. However, there is nothing negative in the desserts in this chapter, unless it is an overload of luscious, scrumptious end-of-the-meal dishes. Here we find the kind of "just desserts" that good cooks have been serving to family, friends, and guests for ages. A richly deserved all-time winner is "Old-Fashioned Vanilla Ice Cream." Everyone will say "I declare . . ." after trying "Ida Claire's Eclairs," an old-fashioned treat if ever there was one.

For cooks who love to try something new, we've included a new twist to an old favorite, "The New Banana Pudding," a yummy no-cook concoction. All recipes here are absolutely great. The cook who serves "Strawberry Dessert," "Tennessee Berry Crisp," or "Biscuit Pudding" can rest assured that the guests have been treated to a finale as rich as a king's ransom!

· *The New Banana Pudding* ·

12 Twinkies
3 bananas
1 6-ounce box instant French vanilla pudding
  Milk
1 4-ounce carton Cool Whip, thawed

Split Twinkies lengthwise; place cream-side up in bottom of a 15x9x2-inch cake pan. Peel bananas and slice; cover top of Twinkies with sliced bananas. Prepare pudding; pour over top of bananas. Spread to cover. Spread Cool Whip over top of pudding. Cover and chill, allow enough time before serving to let the flavors meld together. Cut into squares and serve . . . dee-lishus!!
Makes 12 servings.

■ *Ida Claire's Eclairs* ■

These eclairs were so named because whenever they were served everyone was reported to have cried, "I declare this is the best eclair I've ever tasted."

Pastry

½ cup water
½ stick butter
¼ teaspoon salt
½ cup all-purpose flour
2 eggs

Preheat oven to 400°. Bring water, butter and salt to a boil in a saucepan over medium heat. Add flour all at once, stirring constantly until dough leaves sides of pan and forms a ball. Remove from heat and beat in eggs one at a time (dough will be stiff and glossy). Put dough into a pastry bag. To form eclairs, draw the tube along for 3 to 4 inches on a greased baking sheet. Continue until sheet is filled. Bake for 30 minutes, or until golden brown. Remove from oven and slice along side to allow steam to escape. If dough is not done, return to oven for 5 more minutes. Remove to rack and carefully slice top off each. Remove any uncooked dough and cool completely.

Filling

½ cup milk
1 6-ounce package semi-sweet
  chocolate morsels
1 egg
  Pinch of salt
¼ cup sugar
1 teaspoon vanilla
¼ cup Jack Daniel's Whiskey
1 cup heavy cream

In a small saucepan, scald milk. Place chocolate morsels, egg, salt, sugar and vanilla in blender; pour scalded milk over. Cover blender; blend on low speed for 1 minute. Remove from blender to a bowl; gently stir in Jack Daniel's Whiskey. Cover and chill for 2 hours. Before serving, whip the cream; fold the custard into the whipped cream.

Icing

1 cup confectioners' sugar
⅓ cup cocoa
1 tablespoon butter, melted
2 tablespoons Jack Daniel's
  Whiskey
2 to 3 tablespoons boiling water

In small bowl, combine sugar, cocoa, melted butter and Jack Daniel's Whiskey. Add enough boiling water, by the tablespoon, to make thin glaze. Chill.

TO SERVE: When ready to serve eclairs, assemble by spooning custard filling into pastry, cover with pastry top, drizzle with the icing and then just sit back to hear: "I declare . . .

Makes 8 servings.

▪ *Chocolate Fondue* ▪

We always use this recipe for Super Bowl Sunday. Serve it in a chafing dish with hunks of angel food or pound cake, sliced bananas, apples and strawberries.

1 cup sugar
¾ cup cocoa
½ cup milk
1 14-ounce can sweetened condensed milk
½ stick butter
1 teaspoon vanilla
2 tablespoons Jack Daniel's Whiskey

Combine in order given. Bring to a boil over medium heat. Remove to chafing dish to keep warm. Enjoy!
Makes 3 cups.

Dr. A. Frank Glass

▪ *Surprising Pumpkin Squares* ▪

This recipe was given to me by a great friend, Betty Hutchenson of Tullahoma, Tennessee. It is good all the time, but really nice at Christmas. It goes well with everything.

1 cup sifted self-rising flour
½ teaspoon ground cinnamon
1 stick butter, softened
1½ cups sugar
1 egg
¾ cup mashed pumpkin
¼ cup instant mashed potatoes
½ cup chopped pecans
Confectioners' sugar

Preheat oven to 350°. Sift flour and cinnamon; set aside. Beat butter, sugar and egg in large bowl with electric mixer on high speed until light and fluffy. Stir in pumpkin and potatoes. Stir in flour mixture, a little at a time. Fold in pecans. Pour into greased pan. Bake for 40 minutes. Sprinkle with confectioners' sugar.
Makes 9 servings.

Gina Matherley

▪ *Tennessee Berry Crisp* ▪

Crisps are old-fashioned desserts, but are always a pleaser. This fresh berry one is yummy!

¾ cup quick-cooking rolled oats
¾ cup packed brown sugar
¼ cup all-purpose flour
¼ teaspoon salt
½ stick butter or margarine
1 quart fresh blackberries or raspberries, washed and hulled
2 tablespoons sugar

Preheat oven to 350°. In medium bowl, combine oats, brown sugar, flour and salt. Cut in butter until mixture resembles coarse crumbs; set aside. Place berries in a 10x6x2-inch baking dish. Sprinkle with sugar. Sprinkle crumb mixture on top. Bake for 40 to 45 minutes. Serve warm with cream or ice cream.
Makes 6 servings.

Margaret Tolley

▪ *Harvest Bars* ▪

½ cup solid shortening
1 cup packed brown sugar
⅔ cup pumpkin, cooked and mashed
2 eggs
½ teaspoon vanilla
½ cup chopped dates
½ cup chopped walnuts
2 tablespoons all-purpose flour
½ cup all-purpose flour
½ teaspoon baking powder
¼ teaspoon baking soda
½ teaspoon salt
½ teaspoon cinnamon
½ teaspoon ginger
½ teaspoon nutmeg
  Confectioners' sugar

Preheat oven to 350°. In a 2-quart saucepan, melt shortening. Add brown sugar; stir to blend. Remove from heat. Add pumpkin, eggs and vanilla; mix thoroughly. Combine dates, walnuts and 2 tablespoons flour; set aside. In another bowl, mix dry ingredients, except confectioners' sugar. Add dry ingredients to pumpkin mixture. Blend well. Stir in dates and nuts. Pour into a well-greased 9x9x2-inch pan. Bake for 30 to 35 minutes. Cut into diamond-shaped bars; sift confectioners' sugar over top.

Makes 2 dozen.

Linda Schade

▪ *Sautéed Apples with Jack Daniel's Whiskey and Cinnamon Ice Cream* ▪

Chris Hamilton was formerly a pastry chef at the Hudson River Inn & Conference Center in Ossining, New York. This dessert was always the most popular. She now has her own dessert catering firm called "Grand Finales."

4 pounds apples (about 12)
½ cup lemon juice
6 tablespoons butter
1 vanilla bean
1 cup sugar
  Grated peel from 1 lemon
3 cinnamon sticks
1 cup Jack Daniel's Whiskey
¾ cup heavy cream
  Cinnamon Ice Cream (recipe follows)

Cut and peel apples (about ¼-inch thick); toss with lemon juice. Set aside. Melt butter. Cut and scrape vanilla bean. Cook in butter until the butter starts to brown. Add apples, toss to coat with butter; add sugar and lemon peel. Raise heat to high; add cinnamon sticks and cook until juices are released, then reduce heat. Apples should be almost dry (15 to 20 minutes). Add Jack Daniel's Whiskey. Cook a few minutes to let whiskey evaporate. Add cream. Cool mixture; remove vanilla bean and cinnamon sticks. *Note:* If you wait too long to add the sugar you will get applesauce. You might want applesauce, but I like it with whole slices. The vanilla bean is very important for better flavor. This is a good filling for turnovers—either with pie dough or puff pastry. Serve warm with cinnamon ice cream for a perfect fall/winter dessert.

Makes 8 to 10 servings.

Chris Hamilton

Cinnamon Ice Cream

1 quart light cream
1 cup sugar
10 cinnamon sticks

Bring all ingredients to a boil stirring until sugar is dissolved. Remove from heat and steep (like tea) until you taste a nice strong cinnamon flavor. Discard cinnamon sticks. Chill, then freeze in ice cream freezer. Powdered cinnamon will never match the flavor of a cinnamon stick. No egg yolks in the mix make for a light-colored ice cream that tastes rich but doesn't feel rich in the mouth. At the hotel, I used to let a pot of light cream and cinnamon simmer (covered) for about ½ hour, but if you aren't in a hurry you can just let it steep for an hour or so. No vanilla to mask the pure taste of cinnamon.

■ Chocolate Chess Squares with Jack Daniel's Caramel Sauce ■

1 stick butter
2 squares unsweetened chocolate
4 tablespoons all-purpose flour
2 eggs, slightly beaten
1 cup sugar
½ cup chopped pecans
1 teaspoon vanilla
  Jack Daniel's Caramel Sauce
  (recipe follows)
  Whipped cream

Preheat oven to 350°. Melt butter and chocolate together over low heat. Remove from heat and set aside while mixing flour, eggs, sugar, nuts and vanilla. Combine with chocolate mixture. Pour into a well-greased 8x8-inch square pan. Bake for 20 to 25 minutes. Cool. Cut into squares to serve. Top with Jack Daniel's Caramel Sauce and whipped cream.

Makes 9 servings.

Louise Gregory

Jack Daniel's Caramel Sauce

1 cup sugar
½ cup buttermilk
1 stick butter
½ teaspoon baking soda
1 tablespoon light corn syrup
2 to 3 tablespoons Jack Daniel's
  Whiskey

Combine sugar, buttermilk and butter in saucepan. Bring to a boil, stirring constantly. Boil several minutes until sugar is melted and mixture has thickened. Remove from heat and cool slightly. Add soda and corn syrup. Cool to room temperature; add Jack Daniel's Whiskey.

107

Winning $2,500 is reason to celebrate in anybody's book. These two winners, however, won in a competition of winners. The Jack Daniel's International World Championship Barbecue was a cookoff of champions. Everyone turned out to celebrate and there was fun for all—from the greased pole climb to the country dog contest.

■ Old-Fashioned Vanilla Ice Cream ■

Each Fourth of July family and friends gather at our house for a cookout followed by fireworks. Part of this tradition is serving delicious homemade ice cream along with peach and blackberry cobblers. Our guests must enjoy this tradition because the crowd keeps getting bigger every year.

4 eggs
2¼ cups sugar
1 quart heavy cream
1½ tablespoons vanilla
½ teaspoon salt
5 cups milk

Beat eggs with electric mixer on medium speed until frothy. Gradually add sugar, beating until mixture becomes thick (about 5 minutes). Add remaining ingredients; mix well. Pour into freezer can of a 1-gallon freezer; freeze according to manufacturer's instructions. Let ripen at least 1 hour.

Makes 4 to 6 servings.

Peggy Gray

■ Chocolate Ice Cream ■

2 cups sugar
6 eggs
1 14-ounce can sweetened
   condensed milk
½ pint heavy cream, unwhipped
2 quarts milk
1 cup marshmallows
8 Milky Way candy bars

Beat together sugar and eggs. Add condensed milk, cream and milk. With small amount of milk, melt marshmallows and Milky Ways. Mix everything together and pour into freezer container. Freeze according to manufacturer's directions. This is best if placed in freezer for several hours or overnight before serving.

Makes 1 gallon.

Tana Shupe

108

■ *Authentic Mexican Flan* ■

This recipe is easy and quick, but is fantastic . . . if what you like is the Authentic Mexican Flan. We got this recipe from friends who live in Mexico.

1 14-ounce can sweetened
   condensed milk
1 cup water
6 eggs, well beaten
1 tablespoon vanilla
1 cup sugar

Preheat oven to 350°. Mix milk and water together. Add beaten eggs and vanilla. Melt sugar in a heavy pan until caramel colored. When sugar is completely liquid, pour into a deep pie pan. Pour milk and egg mixture over melted sugar. Set in a pan of water. Bake for 30 minutes or until knife inserted in center comes out clean.
   Makes 6 to 8 servings.

Rhetta McAllister

■ *Fruit Trifle* ■

1 small yellow cake, broken into
   pieces
⅓ cup Jack Daniel's Whiskey
1 cup fruit (cherries, pineapple,
   raspberries, etc.), drained
1 6-ounce box gelatin, prepared as
   directed and chilled until
   thickened, but not firm
1 3½-ounce package vanilla
   pudding, prepared as directed
1 cup whipped cream or
  1 4-ounce carton Cool Whip
  Grated chocolate or fruit

Place pieces of cake in the bottom of a large glass bowl. Sprinkle with Jack Daniel's Whiskey. Place drained fruit on top. Pour cooled gelatin over fruit; chill until firm. Pour the vanilla pudding over gelatin. Top pudding with whipped cream. Decorate with grated chocolate or pieces of fruit. This is best served in a glass bowl so you can see the separate layers.
   Makes 6 servings.

Dawn Weselin

■ *Double Shot Whiskey Pudding* ■

2 cups chopped pitted dates
1 cup Jack Daniel's Whiskey
1¾ cups sugar
2 cups chopped pecans
6 eggs, separated and whites
   beaten stiff
6 tablespoons all-purpose flour
2 teaspoons baking powder
¼ teaspoon salt
  Whipped cream

Several hours or the night before making the pudding, soak the dates in the Jack Daniel's Whiskey. By the time you get ready to make the pudding, dates will have absorbed just about all the whiskey. Preheat oven to 350°. Add sugar, nuts and egg yolks. Add flour sifted with baking powder and salt. Mix well; fold in stiffly beaten egg whites. Pour into buttered ring mold. Bake for 1 hour. (It is best to place mold in a pan filled ½-inch deep with water.) Unmold and serve with whipped cream.
   Makes 8 servings.

Sarah Reese

109

▪ *Pecan Praline-Maple-Jack Daniel's Whiskey Ice Cream* ▪

Pecan Pralines

1 cup sugar
⅓ cup water
1½ cups lightly toasted pecan
   pieces

In a heavy bottomed saucepan, heat the sugar and water until mixture is a light caramel color. Add pecans, stir until well coated. Turn out onto a buttered marble slab or cookie sheet. Let cool. Pulverize brittle and reserve.

Ice Cream

7 large egg yolks
½ cup sugar
2 cups milk
1 cup heavy cream
1 vanilla bean, split
¾ cup maple syrup
¼ cup Jack Daniel's Whiskey

Beat yolks with sugar until pale yellow. In a saucepan, heat milk, cream and vanilla bean to a boil. Remove from heat; slowly whisk into egg yolks. Remove vanilla bean. Place over heat; whisk constantly until slightly thickened. Remove from heat. Add maple syrup and Jack Daniel's Whiskey; chill. When cold, stir in Pecan Pralines and freeze according to manufacturer's directions.
   Makes 1 quart.

▪ *Biscuit Pudding* ▪

Since 1956, Moore County has held a county 4-H camp at Camp Woodlee, near McMinnville, Tennessee. This recipe is a favorite among the adult and teen leaders that attend this camp. It's made from the leftover biscuits Saturday morning and served for lunch.

8 biscuits
½ cup packed brown sugar
¾ cup granulated sugar
2 eggs
1½ cups milk
1 teaspoon vanilla
1 stick margarine or butter
   Whipped cream or ice cream

Preheat oven to 425°. Break biscuits in half, place in iron skillet, soft-side up. Sprinkle brown sugar over biscuits; sprinkle granulated sugar over brown sugar. Beat eggs, add milk and vanilla. Pour over biscuits. If this is not enough liquid to nearly cover biscuits, add enough milk to do so. Cut up margarine; place on top of biscuits. Bake for 30 minutes or until brown. Serve warm with ice cream or whipped cream. This recipe may be varied by the addition of raisins, nuts or a little of our local flavoring, Jack Daniel's Whiskey.
   Makes 8 servings.

Mary Ruth Hall

Lynchburg Hardware and General Store

Tommy Sullenger

If any man in Lynchburg can be credited with a good fish story, it would have to be Tommy Sullenger. Fishing is pastime, pleasure, and real business to him.

Growing up in Hurdlow, a community in Moore County right on the river, Tommy started fishing when he was just a boy. Now, as a professional bass fisherman, he fishes the Tri-Lakes Tournament Trail and the American Team Bass Tournament Trail. Celebrations in the Sullenger household center around tournament winnings . . . with a trophy as the centerpiece for the table.

Fishing takes full-time training. This training quite frequently makes for special occasions. In fact, every Monday and Wednesday, Tommy gets together with other fishermen at nearby Tims Ford Lake for a mini-competition. Everyone gathers at the local restaurant and pitches an entry fee into a pot. The winner for the day who catches the fish that weighs-in the heaviest goes home with the entry pot as his prize.

Eighteen years ago Tommy married Debbie, who was only sixteen at the time. They now have two sons, Matthew and Mark, both budding fishermen. Everything in the family revolves around either fishing or hunting for the guys. Debbie goes along for the ride. She reads a book and then cooks the catch of the day.

For the past ten years, Debbie has worked at the Jack Daniel Distillery. Tommy manages the Lynchburg Hardware and General Store, which sells everything from hogwashers to weather rocks. He is the man to see if you need fly rods or tripods, and if he doesn't have it, he knows who does. One thing's for sure, Tommy has plenty of great fish stories in store. You might bring your own if you drop in—it is the one thing in the store he is always willing to swap.

• *Ginger Peachy Shortcake* •

Shortcakes

1½ cups all-purpose flour
¾ teaspoon salt
½ cup lard or solid shortening
¼ cup ice water
  Cinnamon sugar

Preheat oven to 350°. In mixing bowl, blend flour and salt; cut in lard with pastry cutter or with fingers. Mix until dough resembles coarse corn meal. Add ice water and mix; form dough into a ball. Roll out on lightly floured board. With large round cookie cutter, cut 6 circles of pastry. Place on cookie sheet and sprinkle cinnamon sugar lightly on top. Bake for 10 to 15 minutes or until lightly browned. Remove from oven to cool.

Ginger-Peachy Topping

¾ cup packed brown sugar, divided
4 tablespoons butter
6 large peaches, peeled and sliced
2 tablespoons crystallized ginger
½ cup Jack Daniel's Whiskey
  Sweetened whipped cream

Place half the sugar in a 12x8-inch glass baking dish; dot with 2 tablespoons of butter. Place peach slices on top; sprinkle with ginger. Layer remaining brown sugar; dot with remaining butter. Carefully pour Jack Daniel's Whiskey over all. Bake for 20 minutes.

TO ASSEMBLE: Place a shortcake circle on a plate. Top with Ginger-Peachy topping. Garnish with a dollop of sweetened whipped cream. Can be eaten hot or cold.
  Makes 6 servings.

• *Chuck Wagon Cobbler* •

This recipe is an oldie—but it is still popular because it is quick, easy and always a pleaser. If company shows up at the last hour, stir this up using whatever fruit you have on hand. By the time you have finished eating and are ready for dessert, the cobbler is done.

1 stick butter or margarine
1 cup sugar
1 cup self-rising flour
1 cup milk
  Pinch of salt
1 20-ounce can of any fruit

Preheat oven to 350°. Place stick of butter in a 1½-quart baking dish and place in oven to melt butter. In a mixing bowl, combine sugar, flour, milk and salt. Stir to mix well. Remove baking dish from oven and pour mixture over melted butter—do not stir. Pour can of fruit (juice and all) on top—once again, do not stir. Bake for about 45 minutes to 1 hour. Dough will be done and golden brown on top. Spoon hot into dessert bowls and top with cream, whipped cream or ice cream if desired, and serve. Delicious!
  Makes 6 to 8 servings.

• *Tennessee Whiskey Whip* •

½ pound marshmallows
½ cup Jack Daniel's Whiskey
24 macaroons
1 pint heavy cream, whipped until
    stiff
  Vanilla ice cream
  Maraschino cherries

Cut marshmallows into small chunks. Soak in Jack Daniel's Whiskey for 1 hour. Crumble macaroons. Fold all ingredients together. Chill. To serve, spoon into individual dishes and top with ice cream and a cherry.
Makes 8 to 12 servings.

Ruth Daniel

• *Strawberry Shortcake* •

2 cups sifted all-purpose flour or
    whole-wheat pastry flour
1 tablespoon baking powder
1½ tablespoons sugar
½ teaspoon salt
⅓ cup butter or margarine
¾ cup milk
  Melted butter
3 cups strawberries
1 cup heavy cream
1 teaspoon vanilla
1 tablespoon confectioners' sugar
½ cup sugar

Preheat oven to 425°. In a large bowl, sift first 4 ingredients together. Cut in butter with a pastry blender or two knives. Make a well in center; stir in milk. Stir briefly to mix. Turn onto a floured board; knead gently and briefly. Divide into 2 equal parts and roll and pat each one to the size of an 8-inch round cake pan. Place first layer in pan, brush with melted butter; place second layer over it. Bake for 15 to 20 minutes. Let cool in pan 15 minutes; remove and finish cooling on a wire rack.

Stem and slice strawberries, reserving 10 to 15 beautiful ones for garnish. Just before serving, whip cream with vanilla and confectioners' sugar. Sprinkle sliced strawberries with ½ cup sugar; mix gently. Place bottom half of shortcake on serving plate; spread with about half the whipped cream and all the sliced strawberries. Add top layer, remaining whipped cream and reserved berries, halved or whole.
Makes 4 to 6 servings.

Gloria Shelton

• *Strawberry Dessert* •

1 large angel food cake, crumbled
1 6-ounce and 1 3-ounce box
    instant vanilla pudding
1 4-ounce carton Cool Whip
1 quart strawberries
1 jar strawberry glaze, use as
    much as needed

Crumble cake; place in bottom of large dish or trifle bowl. Mix instant pudding according to directions; pour over cake. Spread Cool Whip over pudding. Wash and hull strawberries. Pat dry with paper towels. Place on top of Cool Whip. Cover all with glaze and chill until serving time.
Makes 12 to 16 servings.

Verna Steelman

113

· CAKES ·

Cakes and celebrations go together. That is why we have birthday cakes, wedding cakes, Christmas cakes, and more. At just about every special occasion cakes are there in loafs or in cups, in bundts or in tubes, in layers or in sheets. Cakes are there vying for attention . . . and being eyed by one and all.

Cakes star at parties to complement tea or coffee. Cakes are the centerpieces for wedding receptions or anniversary celebrations. A cake is a spectacular finale for any occasion. If it is light as air, we call it angel food cake; if it is rich and dense, we call it pound cake. Cakes come in all manner of ways, from upside down to dumped and crazy. Iced or frosted, cakes are a tempting confection; plain or topped with cream, they are no less a temptation.

Cooks are thrilled to hear *ooohs* and *aaahs* over their creations. Any effort that they have made (and sometimes it is considerable) is worth it when praises are sung about their glorious cakes. Every cook seems to have a favorite cake, which is why we received more cake recipes than any other kind for this book. We couldn't include them all and had to leave out many delicious cakes. The collection that is here is an outstanding one for the most discriminating cook.

▪ *German Strawberry Cake* ▪

This is the recipe for my birthday cake made each year by my mom, Shirley Lewis of Mulberry, Tennessee. It has become a family favorite.

1 18.25-ounce box white cake mix
1 6-ounce box strawberry-flavor
   gelatin
1 cup vegetable oil
½ cup milk
1 cup chopped nuts
1 cup strawberries, mashed
4 eggs, beaten
1 cup coconut
¾ box confectioners' sugar
1 stick butter, melted
½ cup nuts
½ cup strawberries, mashed
½ cup coconut

Preheat oven to 350°. Combine first 8 ingredients. Pour into a greased tube pan. Bake for about 1 hour or until skewer inserted in center comes out clean. (Can be baked in layers, if desired.) Combine remaining ingredients and frost cooled cake.
   Makes 1 cake.

Brenda Lewis Graham

▪ *Butter Rum Cake* ▪

This recipe for Butter Rum Cake is from Recipes for Living *by Mrs. R. G. LeTourneau. I found this in the little magazine* LeTourneau NOW, *May 1975. I use this any time I need a cake. It keeps well in the refrigerator or can be frozen.*

1 18.25-ounce box butter cake mix
1 3-ounce box instant vanilla
   pudding
½ cup vegetable oil
4 eggs, beaten
1 cup water
1 teaspoon rum flavoring
   Butter Rum Syrup (recipe
   follows)

Preheat oven to 350°. Mix all ingredients, except Butter Rum Syrup. Pour into a greased and floured tube or bundt pan. Bake for 45 to 50 minutes. While cake is still in pan, pour syrup over it. Let set in pan for 30 minutes.
   Makes 1 cake.

Lucille B. Kelly

Butter Rum Syrup

1 stick margarine
1 cup sugar
⅓ cup water
½ teaspoon rum flavoring

Place all ingredients, except flavoring, in small saucepan. Bring to a boil. Cook until sugar is dissolved. Add flavoring. Pour hot syrup on cake.

■ *Perfect Chocolate Cake* ■

1 cup unsifted unsweetened cocoa
2 cups boiling water
2¾ cups sifted all-purpose flour
2 teaspoons baking soda
½ teaspoon salt
½ teaspoon baking powder
1 cup butter or margarine,
   softened
2½ cups sugar
4 eggs
1½ teaspoons vanilla
   Mock Whip Cream Filling (recipe
   follows)
   Frosting (recipe follows)

In a medium bowl, combine cocoa with boiling water; mix with wire whisk until smooth. Cool completely. Sift flour with soda, salt and baking powder. Preheat oven to 350°. Grease well and lightly flour three 9x1½-inch layer cake pans. In a large bowl, beat butter, sugar, eggs and vanilla with electric mixer on high speed, scraping bowl occasionally, until light, about 5 minutes. On low speed, beat in flour mixture ¼ at a time, alternately with cocoa mixture ⅓ at a time, beginning and ending with flour mixture. Do not overbeat. Divide evenly into pans; smooth tops. Bake for 25 to 30 minutes, or until surface springs back when gently pressed with fingertips. Cool in pans 10 minutes. Carefully loosen sides with spatula; remove from pans; cool on racks. Use Mock Whip Cream Filling between layers. Frost cake and store, covered, in refrigerator.
   Makes 1 cake.

Martha Peay

Mock Whip Cream Filling

1 stick butter
½ cup solid shortening
1 cup sugar
3 tablespoons all-purpose flour
⅔ cup milk
1 teaspoon vanilla

In a large mixing bowl, beat the butter and shortening with electric mixer on high speed until very creamy. Add sugar and flour gradually, beating constantly for a smooth creamy texture. Turn the speed down so the milk will not splatter, then gradually mix in milk and vanilla. Then, turn the speed up again and beat for 5 minutes on high or until smooth and creamy.

Frosting

1 6-ounce package semi-sweet
   chocolate morsels
½ cup light cream
2 sticks butter or margarine
2½ cups unsifted confectioners'
   sugar

In a medium saucepan, combine chocolate morsels, cream and butter. Stir over medium heat until smooth. Remove from heat. With whisk, blend in 2½ cups confectioners' sugar. In bowl, set over ice, beat frosting until it holds its shape. Frost top and sides of cake.

• *Texas Sheet Cake* •

This cake is absolutely a favorite. It is the cake I took to every church social when I was young because it is so easy and is the first cake to disappear. Although the name is simple, it could be called "Better Than Brownies" because it is!

2 cups all-purpose flour
2 cups sugar
1 stick butter or margarine
½ cup solid shortening
3½ tablespoons cocoa
1 cup water
½ cup buttermilk
1 teaspoon baking soda
2 eggs
1 teaspoon vanilla
1 stick butter or margarine
3½ teaspoons cocoa
6 tablespoons milk
1 16-ounce box confectioners' sugar
1 teaspoon vanilla
1 cup chopped pecans

Preheat oven to 400°. Mix flour and sugar in large bowl. Combine 1 stick margarine, shortening, 3½ table-spoons cocoa and water in a saucepan; bring to a boil. Remove from heat. Pour cocoa mixture over flour mixture and mix well. Add buttermilk, soda, eggs and 1 teaspoon vanilla; beat well to mix. Pour batter into a greased and floured 16x11-inch jelly-roll pan. Bake for 20 minutes. While cake is baking, combine the next 4 ingredients in a saucepan and place on low setting on stove, stirring occasionally to mix well. Remove cake from the oven. Stir vanilla and pecans into frosting mixture. Blend well. Pour over hot cake. Delicious!

Makes 1 cake.

Doris Lynch

• *Joy Cake* •

This is a very old recipe that my mother, Ruth Overstreet, often made for her family. Once she made the cake and her son, Robert, grumbled when he found that she had again made Joy Cake. She asked him why he acted that way about dessert. He replied, "I would be a lot happier if we didn't always have to have "Joy Cake!"

3 1-ounce squares dark chocolate
½ cup hot water
½ cup solid shortening
1⅔ cups sugar
3 eggs
2 cups all-purpose flour
3 teaspoons baking powder
½ teaspoon salt
1 cup sour milk
½ teaspoon baking soda
Chocolate Icing (recipe follows)

Preheat oven to 350°. Shave chocolate and add to hot water; heat slowly. Set aside. Cream shortening and sugar until light and fluffy; beat in eggs. Sift flour with baking powder and salt; add to batter alternately with sour milk and soda. Add chocolate mixture; blend well. Grease and flour two 9-inch cake pans. Pour batter into pans. Bake for about 25 minutes or until a skewer inserted in center comes out clean. Remove from oven and cool on wire racks. Spread icing between layers and then frost top and sides of cake.

Makes 1 cake.

Wildred Patton

Chocolate Icing

6 tablespoons solid shortening
1 egg yolk
3 cups confectioners' sugar
4 tablespoons cocoa
2 tablespoons hot water

Cream shortening with egg yolk; blend in sugar and cocoa, alternately with hot water. Beat until smooth.

■ Molasses Cake ■

My grandmother gave this recipe to me years ago. She grew up in Moore County and lived to be 96 years old. She was a wonderful person and a very good cook. She would make this cake for us and keep it in her old pie safe. It keeps for a long time.

1 stick butter, softened
1 cup plus 2 tablespoons sugar
1 cup all-purpose flour
1 cup molasses
1 teaspoon ginger or 2 tablespoons cocoa
1 egg, separated
1 cup boiling water with 1 teaspoon baking soda dissolved in it

Preheat oven to 325°. Stir butter and sugar together; blend in flour and stir well. Add molasses, ginger and egg yolk; beat well. Add the boiling water; fold in egg white, beaten stiff. Pour into an 8x8-inch biscuit pan. Bake for 30 to 40 minutes or until skewer inserted in center comes out clean.

Makes 1 cake.

Mrs. Charlotte Baker

■ Grandmother's Pound Cake ■

This is my grandmother's recipe. She was a very particular cook and never shared her recipes with anyone. I was able to get several of her recipes after years of asking. She was 86 years old when she did give them to me. This pound cake is a favorite of my Daddy's.

2 sticks butter
1⅔ cups sugar
5 eggs
1½ tablespoons lemon juice
½ teaspoon almond extract
2 cups cake flour, sifted with ½ teaspoon salt

Preheat oven to 325°. Cream butter well; add sugar gradually. Mix until light and fluffy. Add eggs, one at a time, beating well after each addition. Add lemon juice and almond extract, beat well. Add flour and beat well. Pour into a well greased loaf pan (or bundt pan). Bake for 70 minutes. Do not open door during baking. Let cool before taking out of pan. *Note:* If using loaf pan, also line with waxed paper, then grease again.

Makes 1 cake.

Mary Trice

119

• *Sweet Potato Upside-Down Cake* •

I'm sure this cake recipe was more condensed in the original recipe, but the person who gave it to me wrote it this way. When I finished putting it together, I had the whole kitchen to clean up! When I baked it the second time, I spread a small can of mandarin orange slices in the bottom of the pan and the cake portions cut out much better when it was served. I used the liquid in the can to make the sauce. I like to experiment with recipes and change them to suit me.

1 cup water
2¾ cups granulated sugar, divided
3 oranges thinly sliced or 1 8-ounce can mandarin oranges
6 tablespoons butter, divided
¼ cup packed brown sugar
1¼ cups solid shortening
4 eggs, separated
1 teaspoon vanilla
1½ cups grated raw sweet potatoes
1 cup chopped walnuts
2½ cups sifted all-purpose flour
1 tablespoon baking powder
½ teaspoon salt
1 teaspoon cinnamon
1 teaspoon nutmeg
1 tablespoon cornstarch
¼ cup milk

Preheat oven to 325°. Combine water and ¼ cup sugar in saucepan. Bring to a boil; add oranges. Cook over medium heat for 20 minutes. Drain; reserve liquid. Cool; cut each orange slice in half. Melt 4 tablespoons butter in a 13x9x2-inch baking pan. Mix in ¼ cup sugar and brown sugar; spread evenly in pan. Arrange orange slices in three rows lengthwise in pan. Cream shortening in bowl with 2 cups sugar. Beat in egg yolks and vanilla until fluffy. Stir in sweet potatoes and walnuts. Add next 5 ingredients alternately with milk, mixing well after each addition. Fold in stiffly beaten egg whites. Spoon evenly over orange slices. Bake for 1 hour or until a skewer inserted in center comes out clean. Cool in pan for 5 minutes. Add enough water to reserved orange liquid to make 1 cup. Blend in cornstarch and remaining ¼ cup sugar and 2 tablespoons butter. Cook until slightly thickened, stirring constantly. Serve warm over warm cake.

Makes 1 cake.

• *Jack Daniel's Chocolate Birthday Cake* •

1½ cups water
½ cup Jack Daniel's Whiskey
1 tablespoon instant coffee granules
2½ sticks butter
1 cup cocoa
2 cups sugar
2 eggs
2 cups all-purpose flour
2 teaspoons baking powder
⅛ teaspoon salt
1 cup coarsely chopped pecans
2 tablespoons Jack Daniel's Whiskey

Preheat oven to 325°. In a very large saucepan, heat water, ½ cup Jack Daniel's Whiskey, coffee, butter and cocoa until butter melts. Remove from heat; beat in sugar, then eggs. In a bowl, stir together flour, baking powder and salt. Beat into chocolate mixture until incorporated. Stir in pecans. Turn batter into a greased and floured tube pan. Bake about 1 hour, or until a skewer inserted in center comes out clean. Immediately sprinkle with 2 tablespoons Jack Daniel's Whiskey. Cool in pan on a wire rack; remove cake from pan. May be topped with a chocolate glaze or confectioners' sugar.

Makes 1 cake.

▪ *Vanilla Wafer Cake* ▪

2 sticks butter
2 cups sugar
6 eggs
1 12-ounce box vanilla wafers, crushed
1 7-ounce can coconut
1 cup chopped pecans
Cream Cheese Frosting (recipe follows)

Preheat oven to 275°. Cream butter and sugar until light and fluffy. Add eggs, one at a time, beating well after each addition. Add crushed wafers, coconut and nuts. Pour into a greased tube pan. Bake for 1½ hours or until a skewer inserted in center comes out clean. Cool. Frost with Cream Cheese Frosting.

Makes 1 cake.

Barbara Davenport

Cream Cheese Frosting

1 8-ounce package cream cheese
1 stick butter
1 16-ounce box confectioners' sugar
1 teaspoon vanilla
½ cup chopped pecans

Mix cream cheese, butter and sugar until smooth. Stir in vanilla and nuts; blend thoroughly.

▪ *Barbara's Holiday Fruitcake* ▪

2 14-ounce cans sweetened condensed milk
1 cup candied pineapple
2 cups chopped pecans
1½ cups chopped walnuts
¾ to 1 cup candied cherries
1 cup orange slice candy, cut into pieces
1 cup shredded coconut
12 fig newtons
1 cup white seedless raisins
1 teaspoon allspice
1 teaspoon cinnamon
1 teaspoon nutmeg
(or 1 tablespoon of pumpkin pie mix instead of allspice, cinnamon and nutmeg)
2 tablespoons vanilla
2 tablespoons Jack Daniel's Whiskey

Preheat oven to 250°. Combine all ingredients and mix well. Pour into a greased and floured tube pan. Bake for 2½ hours. Make up several weeks ahead of time for the holiday season. Soak cheesecloth in Jack Daniel's Whiskey and wrap cake carefully. Store in box away from heat until needed. You can doctor with more Jack Daniel's Whiskey by wetting cheesecloth as needed in between time of preparation and eating. Hmmm, good until the last crumb is gone!

Makes 1 cake.

Barbara Wright

121

▪ *Lazy Daisy Oatmeal Cake* ▪

Each year for his birthday, my husband requests this oatmeal cake that looks and tastes like a German Chocolate cake. My mother-in-law got the recipe from a Quaker Oats box many years ago and passed the recipe on to me. I have made a few minor adjustments.

1¼ cups boiling water
1 cup Quaker or Mother's Oats (quick or old-fashioned, uncooked)
1 stick butter or margarine, softened
1 cup granulated sugar
1 cup packed brown sugar
1 teaspoon vanilla
2 eggs
1½ cups sifted all-purpose flour
1 teaspoon baking soda
½ teaspoon salt
¾ teaspoon cinnamon
¼ teaspoon nutmeg
1 stick butter or margarine, melted
1 cup packed brown sugar
6 tablespoons milk
⅔ cup chopped nuts
1½ cup shredded or flaked coconut

Preheat oven to 350°. Pour boiling water over oats; cover and let stand 20 minutes. Beat 1 stick butter until creamy; gradually add sugars and beat until fluffy. Blend in vanilla and eggs. Add oat mixture; mix well. Sift together flour, soda, salt, cinnamon and nutmeg. Add to creamed mixture. Mix well. Pour into well-greased and floured 13x9x2-inch pan. Bake for approximately 30 minutes or until skewer inserted in center comes out clean. Do not remove from pan. Combine remaining ingredients. Spread evenly over cake. Place under broiler until frosting becomes bubbly. Cake may be served warm or cold.
  Makes 1 cake.

Peggy Gray

▪ *Egg Nog Cakes* ▪

This recipe was handed down from my grandmother to my mother and then to me. When I was a child, we would make these cakes every Christmas, assembly-line style. My mother would cut the cakes, I would dip and my brother would roll and put them in the tins.

1 loaf-shaped angel food cake
1 stick butter
1 16-ounce box confectioners' sugar
½ cup Jack Daniel's Whiskey
½ pound crushed pecans
½ pound crushed vanilla wafers

Cut angel food cake into 1-inch pieces and set aside. Melt butter; mix with confectioners' sugar until smooth. Add Jack Daniel's Whiskey to dipping consistency (set aside what is not used . . . you will have to add the Jack Daniel's Whiskey as you go along to keep dipping consistency). Mix pecans and vanilla wafers in a large bowl; set aside. Dip cake pieces in dipping mixture until well coated on all sides. Roll in vanilla wafer mixture until well coated. Layer in candy tins and seal. Let stand for at least 3 days.
  Makes approximately 4 to 5 dozen.

Riley Parkhurst

Moore County
High School
Alumni
Association
Annual Dinner
Louise Ervin

Louise Ervin was born in Moore County. She grew up, went to school, married, and reared a family there, and worked at the Jack Daniel Distillery until she retired four years ago. In fact, she has never lived anywhere but Moore County, and so it stands to reason that she's involved with the annual celebration sponsored by the Moore County High School Alumni Association.

Each spring the high school alumni receive a letter from the association reminding them of the upcoming reunion dinner. Louise says she believes there are former students living in every state of the Union. Keeping the mailing list updated is a job in itself, and Louise has been the secretary of the organization since it was begun. Much planning is required for this catered event, which takes place the first weekend in June. Each year about 250 members come from as far away as California, Hawaii, and Maine for the food, fun, and conversation with old friends.

Louise is an active member and clerk of the same church where Jack Daniel himself worshiped. She loves to cook and to garden and is happiest when preparing foods or decorating the tables for church dinners and other social events. Her lovely floral arrangements usually are made up of flowers from her own garden. Many times she takes arrangements to Miss Mary Bobo's Boarding House where she is also a part-time hostess. Whether acting as hostess at the annual alumni dinner, her church socials, or at Miss Mary's, Louise exhibits the grace and gentility for which Southern women are known.

▪ *Butter Pecan Cheesecake with Jack Daniel's Creme Anglaise* ▪

BASE:
2½ pounds cream cheese, softened
¾ cup sugar
7 eggs

Whip cheese and sugar until creamed. Add eggs, one or two at a time, and beat to smooth consistency.

CARAMEL:
1 cup sugar
¼ cup water
¾ teaspoon cream of tartar
2 tablespoons butter
½ cup heavy cream, heated

Bring sugar, water and cream of tartar to a boil. Simmer and reduce to caramel state (golden brown). Whisk in butter, then hot cream and mix until smooth. Set aside.

CRUST:
1 cup graham cracker crumbs
¼ cup pecans
¼ cup brown sugar
¼ cup melted butter

Mix all ingredients well. Press into bottom and sides of a springform pan.

To Assemble: Preheat oven to 300°. Whip base well and slowly add in caramel. Pour on top of crust mixture. Place springform pan on cookie sheet. Bake for approximately 2 hours.

Jack Daniel's Creme Anglaise

1 cup cream
1 cup milk
½ cup sugar
5 egg yolks
1 teaspoon grated orange peel
3 tablespoons Jack Daniel's Whiskey

Scald cream and milk. Mix sugar and egg yolks in a heavy pan. Add orange peel to Jack Daniel's Whiskey; pour into scalded cream. Carefully pour liquid mixture into sugar and egg yolks, stirring constantly (otherwise you'll get scrambled eggs) over low heat. Continue stirring constantly until mixture thickens. *To serve,* spread pool of Creme Anglaise on plate; and place slice of cheesecake on top. *Optional:* Sprinkle top of cheesecake with chopped pecans.

Source: Developed at Dakota's Restaurant in Dallas for the Merchants Restaurant in Nashville by Chef James Severson.

Makes 1 cake.

James Severson

▪ *Jubilee Chocolate Cheesecake* ▪

2 cups chocolate wafer crumbs
6 tablespoons butter, melted
3 tablespoons sugar
3 8-ounce packages cream cheese
1 cup plus 2 tablespoons packed
  light brown sugar
3 tablespoons Jack Daniel's
  Whiskey
2 1-ounce semi-sweet chocolate
  squares, melted
3 eggs
  Chocolate for garnish

Combine first 3 ingredients and mix well. Press firmly into an 8 or 9-inch springform pan. Bake at 325 degrees for 10 minutes. Cool. Preheat oven to 325°. Combine cream cheese, sugar and Jack Daniel's Whiskey Mix until well blended. Add melted chocolate. Add eggs, one at a time, beating well after each addition. Pour mixture into crumb crust. Bake for 35 to 40 minutes. Cool, then chill. Garnish with additional shaved chocolate curls, if desired.

▪ *The Tennessee Whiskey Cake* ▪

Tradition has it that there is a cake that represents each state, such as the New York Cheesecake, the California Sunshine Cake or the Texas Sheet Cake. Well, nothing says Tennessee better than Jack Daniel's Whiskey, and this is the cake that takes the cake for the Great State of Tennessee, the Volunteer State. No matter what state you fix it in, you'll find plenty of volunteers to test the recipe!

6 eggs, separated
2 sticks butter, softened
2 cups sugar
½ cup Jack Daniel's Whiskey
2 cups all-purpose flour
½ teaspoon nutmeg
2½ cups raisins
1½ cups chopped pecans

In a small bowl, beat egg whites until stiff; set aside. In large mixing bowl, cream butter and sugar until light and fluffy. Add egg yolks and beat well; add Jack Daniel's Whiskey and stir to blend. Preheat oven to 300°. Brown the flour in a dry skillet. To brown flour, place it in a skillet and cook over medium heat while stirring until it is pale brown in color. This will make the cake a darker color and will add a slightly nutty flavor to the cake. Stir in nutmeg. Beat flour into creamed ingredients. Fold in egg whites, raisins and pecans. Bake in a greased and floured 9-inch tube pan for about 2½ hours or until skewer inserted in center comes out clean. Let cool or even refrigerate before serving. Serve with ice cream or whipped cream, if desired!
Makes 1 cake.

Birthdays are special days whether you are two or twenty. Gifts and a cake, party hats and streamers, noise makers and candles all add to the fun of the celebration. No matter how big or how small the party is, it's your day and you are made to feel special when family and friends honor you on your birthday.

■ *Granny's Old-Fashioned Real Gingerbread* ■

Both of my grandparents went west on a covered wagon and were there when the Oklahoma Indian Territory was opened for statehood. My grandmother outlived all of her sons, and in her lifetime saw a man walk on the moon. Until the day she died she sang, had a wonderful sense of humor and spread cheer to all around her. In her younger days she was an excellent cook. Life was very hard in pioneer states. However, she taught herself to play the piano and she and all the family sang in wonderful harmony as a way of entertainment in their isolated home. This is a cake that she made often to make their family sings even more special.

½ cup solid shortening
½ cup sugar
1 egg, beaten
2½ cups sifted all-purpose flour
1½ teaspoons baking soda
1 teaspoon cinnamon
1 teaspoon ginger
½ teaspoon cloves
½ teaspoon salt
1 cup molasses
1 cup hot water

Preheat oven to 350°. Cream shortening and sugar; add beaten egg. Measure and sift dry ingredients; add alternately with molasses and hot water to sugar mixture. Beat until smooth. Bake in a greased 9x9-inch pan for 45 minutes or until a skewer inserted in center comes out clean. Nice with applesauce, whipped cream or chocolate frosting.

Makes 1 cake.

(Granny) Ruth Overstreet

126

▪ *Royal Crown Cake* ▪

I make this cake a lot because it is so easy to make and tastes so good.

2 cups unsifted all-purpose flour
2 cups sugar
0 tablespoons cocoa
1 teaspoon baking soda
1 teaspoon salt
2 sticks butter or margarine
1 cup Royal Crown Cola or any
   cola-flavored carbonated
   beverage
½ cup buttermilk
2 eggs
1½ cups miniature marshmallows
   Frosting (recipe follows)

Preheat oven to 350°. Combine flour, sugar, cocoa, soda and salt. Bring the butter and cola to a boil; add to flour mixture. Add the buttermilk, eggs and marshmallows. This will be a very thin batter with the marshmallows floating on top. Bake in 13x9x2-inch pan, for 30 to 40 minutes or until a skewer inserted in center comes out clean. Spread frosting over hot cake.
    Makes 1 cake.

Brenda Knight

Frosting

1 stick butter or margarine
2 tablespoons cocoa
6 tablespoons Royal Crown Cola
1 16-ounce box confectioners'
   sugar
1 cup chopped nuts
1 teaspoon vanilla

Combine butter, cocoa and cola; bring to a boil. Pour over confectioners' sugar; mix well. Stir in nuts and vanilla.

▪ *Chocolate Zucchini Cake* ▪

1 stick plus 1 tablespoon
   margarine, softened
2 cups sugar
3 eggs
2 squares unsweetened chocolate,
   melted
2 teaspoons vanilla
2 teaspoons grated orange peel
½ cup milk
2 cups grated raw zucchini
2½ cups all-purpose flour
2½ teaspoons baking powder
1½ teaspoons baking soda
1 teaspoon salt
1 teaspoon cinnamon

Preheat oven to 350°. In large bowl, cream margarine and sugar together. Beat in eggs. Stir in melted chocolate, vanilla, orange peel and milk. In separate bowl, combine remaining ingredients. Beat into chocolate mixture. Pour batter into a greased and floured 10-inch bundt pan. Bake for about 1 hour or until a skewer inserted in center comes out clean. Cool on wire rack before removing from pan. *Note:* This freezes well. We eat this as is or it can be drizzled with a chocolate glaze.
    Makes 1 cake.

Blanche Parks

127

▪ *Fruit Cocktail Cake* ▪

2 cups all-purpose flour
1½ cups sugar
1 egg
1 tablespoon vegetable oil
1 teaspoon vanilla
1 16-ounce can fruit cocktail
1 stick margarine
1 cup sugar
1 5-ounce can evaporated milk
1 teaspoon vanilla
1 8-ounce can coconut

Preheat oven to 350°. Combine first 6 ingredients. Pour into a 9x12-inch sheet pan. Bake for 30 to 35 minutes or until a skewer inserted in center comes out clean. Set cake aside to cool; pierce holes into cake so icing will penetrate into cake. Combine margarine, 1 cup sugar, evaporated milk and vanilla in saucepan over medium heat. Cook until mixture boils for 1 minute, stirring constantly. Remove from heat, add coconut and pour over cake while warm. A half cup of chopped nuts may be added to icing, if desired. *For an interesting variation:* Substitute a 16-ounce can of peaches except for ¼ cup of the peach juice. Chop peaches in blender; add to cake mixture in place of fruit cocktail. Also add ¼ cup of peach schnapps. Bake as above. In the icing, substitute 3 tablespoons Amaretto liqueur for the vanilla.

Makes 1 cake.

Jim Ramsey

▪ *Blackberry Jam Cake* ▪

My mother, the late Mrs. Miller Bingham of Fosterville, Tenn., baked this cake for Christmas when we were small children. She always used chocolate icing on it. My children wanted it for their birthday cake and now my grandchildren want it for Christmas and birthdays. This recipe is at least 75 to 80 years old. All our family still want the chocolate icing.

1 stick butter
¼ cup solid shortening
2 cups sugar
4 eggs
1 cup nuts
1 cup raisins
3 cups all-purpose flour
1 teaspoon ground cinnamon
1 teaspoon ground cloves
1 teaspoon ground allspice
4 tablespoons cocoa
1 teaspoon baking soda
1 teaspoon baking powder
½ teaspoon salt
1 cup buttermilk
1 cup blackberry jam
1 teaspoon vanilla
Chocolate Icing (recipe follows)

Preheat oven to 350°. Cream butter, shortening and sugar; add eggs, one at a time, beating well after each addition. Mix the nuts and raisins with the flour. Stir well; add spices, cocoa, soda, baking powder and salt. Add the buttermilk. Stir into butter mixture. Stir in jam and vanilla. Pour into a greased tube pan or two 9-inch layer cake pans. Bake until skewer inserted in center comes out clean. Cool. Frost with Chocolate Icing.

Makes 1 cake.

Mrs. Margarette Fulks

When Mule Days were celebrated in the South, the showing and selling of mules was serious business. In Lynchburg this used to be a weekly affair. Today, however, it is more of a fun time with contests and food booths where baked goods, fried pies, hot dogs, burgers, barbecue, and drinks are sold. It is an old-time celebration with old-fashioned fun.

Chocolate Icing

3 cups sugar
1 cup milk
2 tablespoons cocoa
½ stick butter
1 teaspoon vanilla

Mix sugar, milk and cocoa in saucepan. Boil until a firm soft ball is formed when dropped into a cup of cold water. Add butter and vanilla. Beat until it begins to thicken. Spread on top and sides of the cake.

■ German Apple Cake ■

½ cup solid shortening
1 stick butter
2 cups sugar
4 eggs
3½ cups all-purpose flour
1 teaspoon cinnamon
1 teaspoon nutmeg
1 teaspoon allspice
1 teaspoon baking powder
¼ teaspoon salt
1 teaspoon baking soda
1 cup cold water
2½ cups chopped apples
1 8-ounce package chopped dates
1½ cups chopped walnuts

Preheat oven to 350°. Cream shortening, butter and sugar in a mixing bowl. Add eggs, one at a time, beating well after each addition. Sift flour with spices, baking powder, salt and soda. Add to creamed mixture, alternately with water. Stir in apples, dates and walnuts; mix thoroughly. Pour into a well-greased 9-inch tube pan. Bake for 1 hour and 15 minutes or until a skewer inserted in center comes out clean.
   Makes 1 cake.

■ Old-Fashioned Dried Apple Cake ■

2 cups dried apples
4 cups all-purpose flour
1 teaspoon baking soda
1 teaspoon cinnamon
1 teaspoon allspice
1 teaspoon nutmeg
2 sticks butter, softened
2 cups sugar
2 eggs
1 cup buttermilk
1 cup nuts
1 cup raisins
½ pound candied cherries
½ pound candied pineapple
1 cup molasses
1 cup jam

Cut apples up, cover with water and soak overnight; cook in water until tender. Cool. Preheat oven to 350°. Prepare 2 loaf pans by lining with greased waxed paper or foil. Sift next 5 ingredients together; set aside. Cream butter and sugar until light and fluffy. Beat in eggs. Add flour mixture alternately with buttermilk. Fold in nuts, fruit, apples, molasses and jam. Bake for 1 hour or until cake springs back when pressed lightly in center.

Makes 2 loaf cakes.

Arah Holder

■ Miss Pepper's Sho' Lawdy Do Taste Good Christmas Cake ■

Alan Heath is a Tennessean from Westmoreland, Tennessee and has lived in England for 17 years. He teaches at an American school there. He hopes to eventually have a log cabin in Tennessee or Kentucky so he can split his time between living there and in England. He eats at Miss Mary Bobo's every summer when he visits relatives in Kentucky.

2 pounds candied fruit, chopped (cherries, apricots, pineapple, pears, etc.)
1 pound dates, chopped
1 pound flaked coconut
1 pound nuts, broken (pecans, walnuts, hazelnuts, brazils, etc.)
2 14-ounce cans sweetened condensed milk

Preheat oven to 250°F. Mix first 4 ingredients in a large bowl with hands or wooden spoons. (This is a muscle-building activity.) Blend in condensed milk. Butter a bundt pan, ring pan, or angel food cake pan and line with waxed paper, extending paper about one inch beyond top of pan. Then butter the paper. Have a glass of mulled wine. Slowly pack the baking pan with the cake mixture, ensuring that there are no airholes. Press and smooth the top of the mixture with a wooden spoon. Bake for 3 hours. Cool in pan. Invert onto gorgeous Spode serving plate. Serve small slices with eggnog, coffee or tea throughout the holidays. The cake may be sliced and frozen in small parcels. Unlike Miss Pepper's other fruit cakes, which contain flour, this cake does not react well to "seasoning" with spirits.

Makes 1 cake.

Alan Heath

▪ *Vivi's Marble Cake* ▪

Vivian McGeachy, my grandmother, was the best cook I have ever known. This marble cake recipe has been in my family for at least four generations. She always kept a marble cake in her cake tin and one in my family's cake tin.

2 squares unsweetened chocolate, melted
4 tablespoons sugar
⅓ cup water
¼ teaspoon baking soda
1½ sticks butter, softened
2 cups sugar
3 teaspoons baking powder
3 cups cake flour
½ teaspoon salt
¾ cup milk
6 egg whites, beaten until stiff
1 teaspoon vanilla

Melt chocolate. Add 4 tablespoons sugar and water. Cook to a smooth consistency. Stir in soda. Let cool; set aside. Preheat oven to 325°. Cream butter and 2 cups sugar until very light. Combine baking powder, flour and salt; add flour alternately with milk while mixing. Gently fold in egg whites. Add vanilla. Blend 6 large spoonsful of batter into chocolate mixture. Mix well. Line a tube pan with wax paper. Alternate adding cake mixtures to pan, by first putting 4 large spoonsful of white cake mixture into pan, then 4 spoonsful of chocolate mixture. Repeat until all the mixtures have been put into pan. Shake pan gently. Twirl spatula through center of the batter once to create a marble effect. Bake for 45 minutes or until skewer inserted in center comes out clean.

Makes 1 cake.

Caroline Heard

▪ *Pineapple Sheet Cake* ▪

2 cups sugar
2 cups all-purpose flour
½ cup vegetable oil
2 eggs
1 20-ounce can crushed pineapple, with juice
1 teaspoon baking soda
Icing (recipe follows)

Preheat oven to 350°. Combine all ingredients except Icing; mix until well blended. Pour into a well greased 9x13-inch sheet cake pan. Bake for 20 minutes or until a skewer inserted in center comes out clean. If you use an 11x13-inch pan, bake a few minutes longer. Pour Icing over hot cake.

Makes 1 cake.

Served at Miss Mary Bobo's Boarding House

Icing

1 cup sugar
1 stick margarine
⅔ cup evaporated milk
Pinch of salt
½ cup chopped nuts
½ cup coconut

Mix first 4 ingredients in saucepan. Bring to a boil. Lower heat; stir for 10 minutes. Add nuts and coconut.

· PIES ·

Pies are traditionally associated with celebrations. In our childhood pies were used to mark special events such as making a home run, planting a first garden, or earning a merit badge in scouts. Specific pies are associated with specific celebrations so that just the mention of pumpkin pie, mincemeat pie, or cherry pie causes us to think of Thanksgiving, Christmas, or George Washington's birthday. The words *apple pie*—along with such words as *home, mother,* and *the grand old flag*—are used to symbolize everything good about America.

Flaky crusts, luscious creamy fillings with mile-high meringues, or fresh, juicy fruit fillings make pies a truly mouthwatering treat. Pies are for enjoyment and pleasure. Cooks of mother's generation didn't think that cream, milk, or eggs in a crust that was made flaky with butter or lard could be anything less than wonderful.

Pies are rich by today's standards—rich in ingredients and rich in tradition. They are worthy of kings, and cooks still present them royally for special occasions when our lives are to be enriched by the loving preparation of a homemade delicacy to link us with our past.

▪ *Perfect Pie Crust* ▪

When I came to this country there were many dishes with which I was unfamiliar. It didn't take me long, though, to get acquainted with many delicious Southern foods. The only problem was I had to learn how to cook them. Through trial and error I learned how to cook and bake and over the years I acquired an extensive recipe file.

I love all kinds of pies. The following pie crust recipe is easy to make. Why not make several pies? Your family and friends will love you for it.

4 cups all-purpose flour
1 teaspoon baking powder
1 teaspoon salt
1 tablespoon sugar
1¾ cups solid shortening
1 egg, beaten
1 tablespoon vinegar
½ cup cold water

Combine first 4 ingredients: cut in shortening using pastry blender or two knives until mixture resembles coarse meal. Stir in remaining ingredients. Divide dough into 5 equal parts; shape each into a ball and wrap tightly. Chill. May be stored up to 2 weeks in refrigerator. Roll out as needed.

Makes pastry for five 9-inch pies.

Renate Stone

▪ *Chess Pie* ▪

2 sticks butter, at room
 temperature
3 cups sugar
6 eggs
1 tablespoon vinegar
1 teaspoon vanilla
2 unbaked pie crusts

Preheat oven to 325°. Cream butter; add sugar, mixing until well blended. Add eggs, one at a time, beating well after each addition. Stir in vinegar and vanilla. Pour into unbaked pie crusts. Bake for about 30 minutes or until firm in center.

Makes 6 to 8 servings per pie.

Renate Stone

▪ *Easiest Pie Crust In History* ▪

A friend sent us this recipe, but did not include their name. The title was intriguing and so we tried it. Believe us, they were right on target with the name. We've included it so you can share it, too.

1 cup solid shortening or lard
½ cup boiling water
3 cups sifted all-purpose flour
1 teaspoon salt

Beat shortening in the boiling water with a fork until shortening is dissolved. Mix flour and salt; stir into liquid. Roll into a ball and refrigerate for at least 15 minutes. Roll out between sheets of wax paper dusted with flour. For precooked crusts, bake at 400° for 15 to 20 minutes or until golden brown.

Makes two 8-inch crusts or one 12-inch crust.

• *Cocoa Pie* •

This recipe has been handed down from my husband's great-grandmother and is a favorite of my family.

1½ cups milk, divided
1 tablespoon butter
1 cup sugar
⅓ cup cocoa
2 tablespoons cornstarch
Dash of salt
2 eggs, separated
2 teaspoons vanilla
1 9-inch baked pie crust
Meringue (recipe follows)

Heat 1 cup milk and 1 tablespoon butter. Dissolve sugar, cocoa and cornstarch in remaining ½ cup milk. Add salt and well-beaten egg yolks. Pour this mixture into hot milk. Cook until thickened. Stir in vanilla. Pour filling into baked pie crust. Prepare meringue.
Makes 6 to 8 servings.

Terri D. Jennings

Meringue

Reserved egg whites
Cream of tartar
2 tablespoons sugar
½ teaspoon vanilla

Preheat oven to 350°. Add to whites a tiny bit of cream of tartar (less than ⅛ teaspoon). Beat well. Add sugar; beat until stiff peaks form. Blend in vanilla. Spread over pie; seal edges. Brown the meringue slightly in oven.
Makes 6 to 8 servings.

• *Blackberry Cobbler* •

5 cups fresh blackberries, washed and hulled
1¼ cups sugar
¼ cup all-purpose flour
2 tablespoons butter
1 cup all-purpose flour
2 tablespoons sugar
2 tablespoons baking powder
¼ teaspoon salt
½ stick butter
1 egg, slightly beaten
¼ cup milk or cream
Vanilla ice cream

Preheat oven to 400°. Place blackberries in an 8x1½-inch baking dish or 1½-quart casserole. In a small bowl, combine sugar and ¼ cup flour. Sprinkle over blackberries. Dot with 2 tablespoons butter. Set aside. In a large bowl, combine 1 cup flour, sugar, baking powder and salt. Cut in ½ stick butter until mixture resembles coarse crumbs. Combine beaten egg and milk. Add all at once to dry ingredients, stirring just to moisten. Spoon over fruit in 6 mounds. Bake for 20 to 25 minutes or until biscuits are golden brown and fruit is bubbly. Serve warm with vanilla ice cream.
Makes about 6 servings.

Pat Pirkle

135

• *Blackberry Custard Pie* •

*This recipe is more than 100 years old and was made by my
Grandmother Logan and by my mother. It is a delicious custard.*

½ cup all-purpose flour
1½ cups sugar
½ teaspoon salt
4 eggs yolks, beaten
2 cups blackberry juice
1 stick butter or margarine
1 9-inch baked pie crust
4 egg whites
8 tablespoons sugar
¼ teaspoon baking powder or
  cream of tartar

Mix flour, sugar and salt. Add egg yolks, juice and butter. Cook over medium heat until thickened. Pour into pie crust. Preheat oven to 350°. Beat egg whites until very stiff. Fold in 8 tablespoons of sugar, 2 tablespoons at a time. Add baking powder. Spread over pie. Bake until top is brown. *Note:* Grape juice can be substituted for blackberry juice.
Makes 6 to 8 servings.

Dottie Ruth Ashby

• *Lemon Meringue Pie* •

1¼ cups sugar, divided
¼ teaspoon salt
⅓ cup cornstarch
½ cup fresh lemon juice
1½ cups water
1 tablespoon grated lemon peel
3 egg yolks
2 tablespoons butter or margarine
1 9-inch baked pie crust
3 egg whites
¼ teaspoon cream of tartar

Mix together in heavy saucepan: 1 cup sugar, salt and cornstarch. Mix lemon juice, water, and lemon peel. Add to dry ingredients. Add slightly beaten egg yolks. Cook until thickened, stirring constantly. Add butter. Pour into baked pie crust. Preheat oven to 350°. Whip egg whites until frothy; add cream of tartar. Whip until stiff, but not dry, peaks form. Beat in remaining sugar, 1 tablespoon at a time. Spread on pie; seal edges. Slightly brown the meringue in oven.
Makes 6 to 8 servings.

Rada Manley

• *Cider Apple Pie* •

3 cups hard cider
½ pound dried apples
1 cup raisins
¼ teaspoon grated nutmeg
½ teaspoon cinnamon
⅓ cup maple syrup
  Butter
  Pie crust for a 2-crust, 9-inch pie

Preheat oven to 375°. Pour the cider into a medium saucepan; add the apples and raisins. Cook until apples are soft. Add the spices and maple syrup; simmer for 10 minutes. Dot the bottom crust with butter. Pour the apple mixture into the buttered crust; cover with top crust. Cut steam vents in crust. Bake for 40 to 50 minutes or until golden brown.
Makes 6 to 8 servings.

Lonnie Wyrick

136

Freshly caught fish and summer's bounty picked from home gardens are reasons to celebrate in Lynchburg. Food bought in a store just can't compete for flavor and goodness. The pride of the fisherman is seen in his smile and the display of his catch of the day.

▪ *Dad's Favorite Apple Pie* ▪

Pastry for 2-crust 9-inch pie
⅔ cup sugar
⅛ teaspoon salt
¾ teaspoon cinnamon
6 apples, peeled, cored and sliced
Butter
Mom's Secret Sauce (recipe follows)

Preheat oven to 425°. Roll out half of pastry ⅛-inch thick. Place on 9-inch pie pan; prick with fork several times. Combine sugar, salt and cinnamon. Place apples in pie shell; sprinkle sugar mixture over all. Dot with butter. Top with second crust; moisten edges to seal. Cut slits in top of crust to allow steam to escape. Bake for 50 minutes or until top is brown and apples are tender.

Mom's Secret Sauce

3 egg yolks
¾ cup confectioners' sugar
⅛ teaspoon salt
½ teaspoon vanilla
3 tablespoons Jack Daniel's Whiskey
1 cup whipping cream

Beat yolks, then add next 4 ingredients until thick and pale lemon in color. Whip cream until it mounds and hold its shape. Fold into egg mixture; cover and chill. Serve over warm pie—Yummy!

137

▪ *The Easiest, But Best, Key Lime Pie* ▪

1 pint heavy cream, whipped
2 14-ounce cans sweetened
  condensed milk
2 6-ounce cans frozen limeade
  concentrate, thawed
  Green food coloring, optional
2 9-inch graham cracker crumb pie
  crusts

In a cold mixing bowl, whip cream until stiff peaks form. In another bowl, mix sweetened condensed milk and limeade concentrate. With slotted spoon, fold whipped cream into milk mixture. A few drops of food coloring may be added, if desired. Pour into prepared graham cracker crusts. Chill and enjoy!

Makes 6 to 8 servings per pie

▪ *Rum Chiffon Pie* ▪

For years I searched for a Rum Pie recipe to equal that served at the Read House Hotel in Chattanooga, Tennessee. One year at the National Association of Extension Home Economists meeting, the members from Puerto Rico gave us a sample of rum along with a recipe booklet. This is the nearest thing I have ever found to equal that treat at the Read House.

3 eggs, separated
⅓ cup sugar
¼ teaspoon salt
2 cups milk
1 envelope unflavored gelatin
3 tablespoons cold water
6 tablespoons sugar
2 tablespoons 151-proof rum
1 9-inch baked or crumb-type pie
  crust
  Whipped cream
  Unsweetened chocolate

Beat egg yolks slightly. Blend in ⅓ cup sugar and salt. Add milk. Cook in a double boiler over boiling water until thick enough to coat a metal spoon. Soften gelatin in cold water. Add to hot mixture; stir until dissolved. Chill until slightly thickened. Beat egg whites until foamy. Gradually add 6 tablespoons sugar; continue to beat until meringue is stiff. Fold into custard mixture. Fold in rum. Pour into pie crust; chill until firm. Serve with whipped cream garnished with finely shaved unsweetened chocolate.

Makes 6 to 8 servings.

Mary Ruth Hall

▪ *Velvety Custard Pie* ▪

4 eggs, slightly beaten
½ cup sugar
¼ teaspoon salt
1 teaspoon vanilla
2½ cups milk, scalded
1 9-inch unbaked pie crust
  Nutmeg

Preheat oven to 475°. Thoroughly mix eggs, sugar, salt and vanilla. Slowly stir in hot milk. Pour at once into unbaked pie crust. (To avoid spills, fill in oven.) Sprinkle top with nutmeg. Bake for 5 minutes. Reduce heat to 425° and bake 10 to 20 minutes longer or until knife inserted halfway between center and edge comes out clean.

Makes 6 to 8 servings.

Nancy Jennings

▪ *Oatmeal Pie* ▪

This is an old recipe handed down in my family. It used to be referred to as "poor man's pecan pie" since it is a mock pecan pie. Pioneers who didn't have pecans made this pie. It is still a favorite in our house and with the new interest in oatmeal, it is time to reintroduce it to others.

1 cup sugar
2 eggs
1 stick margarine or butter, melted
　Dash of salt
1 teaspoon vanilla
1 cup oatmeal
1 cup dark corn syrup
1 9-inch unbaked pie crust

Preheat oven to 350°. Mix first 7 ingredients together, stirring to blend well. Pour into unbaked pie crust. Bake for 45 minutes or until firm in center. Cool and serve with a dollop of whipped cream, if desired.
　Makes 6 to 8 servings.

▪ *Caramel Pie* ▪

Pie is hard to beat when you want a really special dessert. This pie will take the cake anytime! It is rich and absolutely scrumptious.

1 14-ounce can sweetened
　condensed milk
½ cup packed brown sugar
　Pinch of salt
½ cup coarsely chopped pecans,
　divided
1 cup heavy cream
¼ cup confectioners' sugar
1 9-inch baked pie crust
　Coconut, toasted

In top of double boiler, mix together milk, brown sugar and salt. Cook over rapidly boiling water, stirring until thickened. Remove from heat; stir in half the pecans. Cool to room temperature. In small mixing bowl, whip cream until stiff; fold in confectioners' sugar. Pour filling into cooled pie crust; top with remaining pecans. Spoon whipped cream on top of filling and garnish with toasted coconut. Chill until serving time.
　Makes 6 to 8 servings.

▪ *Chocolate Pecan Pie* ▪

Rich, but oh so good!

3 tablespoons butter, melted
¾ cup sugar
¾ cup light corn syrup
3 eggs
1 cup pecan pieces
1 cup semi-sweet chocolate
　morsels
1 9-inch unbaked pie crust

Preheat oven to 350°. In mixing bowl, combine butter, sugar, syrup and eggs. Mix with electric mixer on medium speed. Stir in pecans and chocolate morsels. Pour into pie crust. Bake for 45 minutes or until center is almost firm. Serve with a scoop of ice cream, if desired.
　Makes 6 to 8 servings.

Wilma Bedford

139

▪ *Pie* ▪

When you make and serve this pie, everyone will think that it is a gourmet pie with lots of fancy ingredients. They will also think that it must be difficult to prepare. They couldn't be more wrong! Believe me, it is the easiest pie to make and the ingredients are simple and few. All of this makes it something spectacular . . . everything that is except its name.

3 egg whites
1 teaspoon baking powder
1 cup sugar
1 cup pecans, chopped
1 cup graham cracker crumbs
1 teaspoon vanilla
½ pint heavy cream
3 tablespoons sugar
1 teaspoon vanilla
Chocolate

Preheat oven to 350°. Beat the egg whites until stiff, adding baking powder while beating. Add 1 cup sugar; gently fold in pecans, graham cracker crumbs and 1 teaspoon vanilla. Pour into a greased pie pan. Bake for 35 minutes or until firm in center. Remove from oven and cool. Combine heavy cream, 3 tablespoons sugar and 1 teaspoon vanilla. Whip until stiff peaks form. Spread on cooled pie and place in refrigerator until serving time. Just before serving, grate chocolate and sprinkle on top.
Makes 6 to 8 servings.

Gale Sutton

▪ *Frozen Jack Daniel's Pecan Pie* ▪

⅓ cup Jack Daniel's Whiskey
2 eggs, separated
½ cup honey
⅛ teaspoon salt
2 teaspoons vanilla
1½ cups heavy cream
¾ cup coarsely chopped pecans
 Nutty Oat Crust (recipe follows)
 Honey-Chocolate Sauce (recipe follows)
 Pecan halves

Combine Jack Daniel's Whiskey, egg yolks, honey, and salt in a small saucepan; stir well. Cook over low heat, stirring constantly, until mixture thickens (do not boil). Remove from heat. Stir in vanilla; let cool completely. Beat egg whites (at room temperature) until stiff but not dry; set aside. Beat cream until soft peaks form. Fold whipped cream and pecans into cooled mixture; fold in beaten egg whites. Spoon into Nutty Oat Crust; freeze 8 hours or until firm. Drizzle with Honey-Chocolate Sauce; garnish with pecan halves, if desired. Serve with remaining sauce.
Makes 6 to 8 servings.

Pamela Fanning

Nutty Oat Crust

1 stick butter or margarine, softened
¼ cup packed light brown sugar
1 cup all-purpose flour
¼ cup regular oats, uncooked
¼ cup finely chopped pecans

Preheat oven to 350°. Cream butter; gradually add sugar, beating well on medium speed with electric mixer. Add flour, oats and pecans; beat on low speed until blended. Press mixture on bottom and 1 inch up sides of a lightly greased 9-inch springform pan. Bake for 20 to 25 minutes or until lightly browned. Cool.
Makes one 9-inch crust.

Honey-Chocolate Sauce

¼ cup plus 2 tablespoons cocoa
1½ tablespoons cornstarch
¼ cup water
¾ cup honey
Pinch of salt
½ stick plus 2 tablespoons butter
or margarine, melted
1 teaspoon vanilla

Combine cocoa and cornstarch in a small saucepan; stir in water, mixing well. Add honey and salt. Cook over medium heat, stirring constantly, until mixture boils; boil 1 minute. Add butter, 1 tablespoon at a time, stirring constantly until melted. Stir in vanilla. Serve at room temperature. Refrigerate leftover sauce for other uses.
Makes 1⅔ cups.

▪ Dot's Chocolate Pie ▪

Some mothers make such good pies that these just have to be shared with others. Such is the case of Judy Mitchell's mom. She makes a great chocolate pie and here is the recipe to prove it.

2 cups sugar
2 tablespoons cornstarch
½ cup cocoa
2 cups milk, divided
5 eggs, separated
½ stick margarine
2 teaspoons vanilla
¼ teaspoon cream of tartar
¼ teaspoon vanilla
½ cup sugar
2 9-inch baked pie crusts

Mix first 3 ingredients together in medium saucepan. Stir in ½ cup milk. Separate eggs. Blend yolks into mixture; slowly add remainder of milk. Bring mixture to a boil over medium heat, stirring constantly. When mixture thickens and begins to boil, remove from heat. Add margarine and 2 teaspoons vanilla. Cool pan by placing in sink of cold water. Preheat oven to 400°. While mixture is cooling, prepare the meringue. Add ¼ teaspoon cream of tartar and ¼ teaspoon vanilla to unbeaten egg whites. Beat until stiff peaks form. Slowly add ½ cup sugar while beating with mixer. Pour cooled chocolate filling into baked pie crusts. Top with meringue. Bake until meringue is golden brown. Cool and serve.
Makes 6 to 8 servings per pie.

Judy Mitchell

▪ Chocolate Chess Pie ▪

1½ cups sugar
3 tablespoons cocoa
2 eggs, slightly beaten
⅔ cup evaporated milk
1 teaspoon vanilla
½ stick butter, melted
1 9-inch pie crust, uncooked
Whipped cream

Preheat oven to 350°. Mix sugar and cocoa. Add eggs, milk, vanilla and butter. Mix well; pour into prepared pie crust. Bake for 45 minutes or until firm. Cool before cutting; garnish with whipped cream.
Makes 6 to 8 servings.

Louise Gregory

141

▪ *Chocolate Angel Pie* ▪

This is my favorite pie—my dad's favorite, too!

2 egg whites
⅛ teaspoon cream of tartar
½ cup sugar
½ cup finely chopped pecans
1 teaspoon vanilla, divided
½ pint heavy cream
4 tablespoons sugar
2 tablespoons cocoa
1 can coconut

Preheat oven to 300°. Beat egg whites until frothy; add cream of tartar and beat until stiff. Gradually add ½ cup sugar, 2 tablespoons at a time. Beat well, sugar should be dissolved. Fold in chopped pecans and ½ teaspoon vanilla. Spoon into glass pie plate that has been sprayed with oil. Make a nest-like shell, building up on the edges. Bake for 50 to 55 minutes. Cool to room temperature.

Whip cream, sugar and cocoa together. Add ½ teaspoon vanilla. Pour into cooled meringue shell; top with coconut. Chill and serve.

Makes 6 to 8 servings.

Alice Bedford

▪ *Chocolate Cheese Pie* ▪

1 stick margarine
1 cup all-purpose flour
1 cup pecans
1 cup confectioners' sugar
1 8-ounce package cream cheese, softened
2 cups Cool Whip, divided
1 4-ounce package instant vanilla pudding
1 4-ounce package instant chocolate pudding
3 cups milk
  Grated chocolate or chocolate bits

Preheat oven to 325°. In a 9x13-inch pan, melt margarine, stir in flour and nuts and pat in bottom of pan. Bake for 20 minutes. Cool completely. Combine confectioners' sugar, cream cheese and 1 cup Cool Whip. Spread on cooled crust. Combine next 3 ingredients; Beat until thick and spread on top of cream cheese layer. Spread remaining Cool Whip on top. Sprinkle chocolate on top, if desired. Voila!!! You have just made a very delicious and fattening dessert.

Makes 6 to 8 servings.

Bette Rogers

▪ *Tennessee Pie* ▪

2 eggs, beaten
1 cup sugar
1 stick butter, softened
¼ cup Jack Daniel's Whiskey
1 teaspoon vanilla
½ cup all-purpose flour
¾ cup semi-sweet chocolate chips
1 cup nuts (black walnuts, pecans or English walnuts)
1 9-inch unbaked pie crust
  Whipped cream

Preheat oven to 350°. Cream together eggs, sugar and butter. Stir in next 5 adding chocolate chips and nuts last. Pour into pie crust. Bake for 35 to 40 minutes. Makes sure crust is nice and brown. Garnish with whipped cream, if desired.

Wilma Early

▪ *Brown Sugar Coconut Pie* ▪

1 pound brown sugar
1 cup granulated sugar
4 tablespoons all-purpose flour
  Dash of salt
1 13-ounce can evaporated milk
1 cup water
6 egg yolks, beaten
½ stick margarine, melted
1 3½-ounce can coconut
1 teaspoon vanilla
3 9-inch unbaked pie crusts
  Meringue (recipe follows)

Preheat oven to 350°. Combine sugars, flour and salt. Add milk and water; mix well. Add egg yolks; beat well. Add margarine and coconut. Cook on top of stove in heavy skillet or saucepan until thick. Stir in vanilla. Pour into pie crusts. Bake for 30 minutes or until pies are firm. Prepare Meringue.

Makes 6 to 8 servings per pie.

Ann O. Tipps

Meringue

6 egg whites
½ teaspoon cream of tartar
6 tablespoons sugar
1 tablespoon vanilla
  Coconut

Preheat oven to 350°. Whip egg whites until frothy, add cream of tartar, whip until stiff, but not dry, peaks form. Beat in sugar, 1 tablespoon at a time. Stir in vanilla. Spread on pies. Sprinkle with a small amount of coconut. Slightly brown meringue in the oven.

Pig racing is a fun event at any fair or festival. It really draws a crowd to cheer the little squealers on. Even the pigs seem to enjoy it because they get Oreo cookies at the end of the race, whether they win or not.

143

▪ Egg Custard Pie ▪

This recipe was given to my daddy by J.B. Husky, owner, operator and well-known good cook of the "Coffee Cup Cafe" located for many years on the Square in Lynchburg.

3 eggs
1¼ cups sugar
1½ tablespoons all-purpose flour
1 stick butter, melted
1 tablespoon cornmeal
1 teaspoon vanilla
¾ cup milk
1 9-inch unbaked pie crust

Preheat oven to 400°. Mix all ingredients together. Pour into unbaked pie crust. Bake for 30 minutes.
Makes 6 to 8 servings.

Terry Ann Noblitt

▪ Brownie Pie ▪

2 squares unsweetened chocolate
1 stick butter
1 cup sugar
¼ cup all-purpose flour
2 large eggs, beaten
¼ teaspoon salt
1 teaspoon vanilla
½ cup chopped pecans
Whipped cream
Maraschino cherries

Preheat oven to 325°. Melt chocolate and butter in a heavy saucepan over low heat. Remove from heat. Combine sugar and flour; stir into chocolate mixture. Add eggs; mix thoroughly. Add salt, vanilla and pecans. Pour into a buttered 9-inch pie pan. Bake for 25 to 30 minutes. Filling should still be moist. Serve warm, topped with whipped cream and maraschino cherries.
Makes 8 servings.

Cathy T. Acuff

▪ Mock Pecan Pie ▪

Bake this and let your guests guess the ingredients. I have tried it many times and no one yet has guessed that it contains pinto beans.

3 eggs
¼ teaspoon salt
2 cups sugar
1 cup mashed cooked pinto beans
1 9-inch unbaked pie crust

Preheat oven to 425°. Beat eggs, salt and sugar together. Add beans; mix well. Let ingredients stand for ½ hour. Pour into pie crust. Bake at 425° until crust begins to brown. Reduce temperature to 375° and bake 30 minutes longer or until firm in center. Serve warm with ice cream or whipped cream, if desired.
Makes 6 to 8 servings.

Mary Ruth Hall

Decoration Day Reunions and Cemetery Celebrations

Wilma and Buck Early

For country folk, family cemeteries are a part of the old homeplace. The problem is that since there is no cemetery staff to clear away the brambles and weeds, the cemeteries are soon overgrown. Cleaning these old cemetery grounds is a perfect opportunity for the family to get together in a joint venture that also celebrates the reuniting of family members. Decoration Day is a favorite time for this. Family members come from far and near, bringing their own delicacies and favorite dishes so that when the work is finished a feast is waiting.

Both Wilma and Buck Early work for the Jack Daniel Distillery. Between them they have fifty-one years of service.

Wilma uses Jack Daniel's Whiskey in a lot of her recipes to give them a special flavor.

Each year on Decoration Day the Earlys travel to Summertown, Tennessee, for Wilma's mother's family reunion and cemetery celebration. She always takes her special "Tennessee Pie," which is flavored with a little of the hometown spirit. It is such a tradition, she says, that she would probably be disinherited if she didn't bring a Tennessee Pie or two. The first thing her Aunt Dickie and Cousin Coon want to know is, "Where is the pie?" This has become such a big deal that Wilma now makes Aunt Dickie her very own pie to take home with her.

▪ *Syrup Pie* ▪

½ cup sugar
1 cup dark cane syrup
¼ teaspoon baking soda
  Pinch of salt
1 stick butter
3 eggs, beaten
1 tablespoon all-purpose flour
  Grated fresh orange peel
¼ cup Jack Daniel's Whiskey
1 9-inch unbaked pie crust

Preheat oven to 325°. Mix sugar, syrup, soda and salt in a saucepan. Bring to a boil, then remove from heat and cool. Stir in butter, beaten eggs, flour, orange peel and Jack Daniel's Whiskey. Pour into unbaked pie crust. Bake for 50 minutes or until firm in center.
  Makes 6 to 8 servings.

▪ *Amber Pie* ▪

3 egg yolks
1 cup sugar
1 tablespoon butter
2 tablespoons all-purpose flour
½ teaspoon cinnamon
¼ teaspoon each cloves, allspice, nutmeg
1 cup buttermilk
½ cup raisins
½ cup pecans
1 9-inch unbaked pie crust

Preheat oven to 325°. Cream egg yolks, sugar and butter until light and fluffy. Add remaining ingredients and blend until smooth. Pour into unbaked pie crust. Bake for 35 to 40 minutes or until firm in center. Can be served warm or cold.
  Makes 6 to 8 servings.

Dorothy Overstreet

▪ *Mama's Chocolate Custard Pie* ▪

Among my favorite Christmas memories is the sight of Mama standing at the stove stirring a big cast-iron skillet, filling the kitchen with the scent of chocolate. Sometimes she'd leave the cocoa out and we'd have what she called egg custard. To many people, the thought of Christmas brings packages and red-suited Santas to mind. But to me, it brings the scent of cedar and a vision of Mama.

3 eggs
1½ cups sugar
3½ cups milk
1 teaspoon vanilla
½ cup all-purpose flour
½ stick butter or margarine
2 tablespoons cocoa
2 baked 9-inch pie crusts

Separate eggs; beat yolks firmly. Add remaining ingredients, except pie crusts and egg whites. Cook over medium heat in a cast-iron skillet, stirring constantly until thickened. Brown pie crusts according to package directions. Pour in filling. Beat egg whites until stiff peaks form. Spread over pie. Brown lightly in oven.
  Makes 6 to 8 servings per pie.

Brenda Ramsey

▪ *Fresh Raspberry Pie* ▪

1 cup sugar
2 tablespoons cornstarch
  Dash of salt
2 pints fresh raspberries
  Pastry for Double Crust Pie
  (recipe follows)
2 tablespoons butter

Preheat oven to 375°. In a large bowl, combine sugar, cornstarch and salt. Add berries to sugar mixture; toss gently to coat fruit. Fill pastry-lined 9-inch pie plate with berry mixture. Dot with butter. Adjust top crust. Seal and flute edge. Bake for 40 to 45 minutes or until crust is golden brown. Cool on wire rack.

Makes 6 to 8 servings.

Pastry for Double Crust Pie

2 cups all-purpose flour
1 teaspoon salt
⅔ cup solid shortening or lard
6 to 7 tablespoons cold water

In a large bowl, combine flour and salt. Cut in shortening with pastry blender or two knives until pieces are the size of small peas. Blend the water lightly into the dough, gently tossing with fork. Divide dough in half, form half into a ball on a lightly floured surface. Roll dough from center to edge forming a circle about 12 inches in diameter. Gently pat pastry into pie plate. For top crust, roll out remaining dough.

▪ *Linda's Strawberry Pie* ▪

2 cups all-purpose flour
2 tablespoons solid shortening
  Milk
3 tablespoons cornstarch
1 cup sugar
½ cup mashed berries
½ cup water
1 tablespoon lemon juice
1 tablespoon butter
  Whole strawberries

Mix flour and shortening with pastry blender or two knives. Add milk until dough is desired consistency. Roll out; place in pie pan. Bake for 15 to 20 minutes or until browned. Combine next 6 ingredients in saucepan; cook until thick. Let cool. Pour over pie crust filled with strawberries.

Makes 6 to 8 servings.

Kathy Woodard

▪ Candies and Cookies ▪

What can satisfy a sweet tooth better than candy? Candies are favorites of everyone, and once a good candy recipe is found, people keep it forever. While some of these recipes are very old, they are still good and popular.

By the same token, cookies are special favorites. Children of all ages love them with milk, as a snack, or as a dessert. They are easy to pack for picnics, lunches, or as a gift to a friend or shut-in. Old favorites like oatmeal and chocolate chip never go out of style. A kitchen fragrant with cookies baking in the oven is a special gathering place, and the cook baking them is loved by all.

▪ *White Fudge* ▪

2 cups sugar
½ cup sour cream
⅓ cup light corn syrup
2 tablespoons margarine
2 teaspoons vanilla

Combine first 4 ingredients in saucepan over medium heat. Cook and stir constantly until candy thermometer reaches 238°. Remove from heat; let stand 15 minutes. Add vanilla; beat until its loses its gloss. Pour into buttered pan. Cool and cut into squares.

Makes 1½ pounds.

Martha Burrus

149

▪ *Granny's Pineapple Cream Candy* ▪

1 cup granulated sugar
½ cup packed brown sugar
¼ teaspoon salt
½ cup water
½ cup crushed pineapple, drained
½ cup chopped nuts
2 tablespoons butter
12 marshmallows, cut into pieces
¼ cup candied cherries
1 teaspoon vanilla

Combine sugars, salt and water; cook to soft ball (238°) stage. Add remaining ingredients; remove from heat. Beat to mix well; cool to room temperature. (You can place pan in sink filled with ice water to cool it faster.) Beat candy until thick and creamy; pour into a buttered pan. Cut into squares when firm.
Makes ½ pound.

Tommy Overstreet

▪ *Peanut Butter Fudge* ▪

Judy is a real candy maker and has shared her three favorite candy recipes with us. She works in the Accounting Department of Jack Daniel's. She has a daughter, Chrissy, who keeps mom very busy cooking up goodies after work.

3 cups sugar
1½ sticks margarine
⅔ cup evaporated milk
1 7-ounce jar marshmallow creme
1 cup creamy peanut butter

Combine sugar, margarine and evaporated milk in a heavy pan. Bring to a boil, stirring constantly. Boil for 5 minutes over medium heat, stirring constantly to keep from scorching. Remove from heat. Add marshmallow creme and peanut butter. Beat well. Pour into lightly buttered dish. Cut into squares when cool.
Makes 8 servings.

Judy Mitchell

▪ *Toffee* ▪

1 cup chopped pecans
¾ cup packed brown sugar
1 stick butter
½ cup semi-sweet chocolate morsels

Butter a 9x9x2-inch pan. Spread pecans in pan. Heat sugar and butter to boiling, stirring constantly. Boil over medium heat for seven minutes, stirring constantly. Immediately spread mixture over nuts in pan. Sprinkle chocolate morsels over hot mixture; cover with baking sheet so contained heat will melt the chocolate. Spread melted chocolate over candy while hot; cut into squares. Chill until firm.
Makes 16 squares.

Judy Mitchell

▪ *Divinity* ▪

2 cups sugar
½ cup light corn syrup
½ cup hot water
¼ teaspoon salt
2 egg whites
1 teaspoon vanilla
½ cup pecans, optional

Combine first 4 ingredients in a 2-quart saucepan. Cook and stir until sugar dissolves and mixture comes to a boil. Cook to hard ball stage (250° on candy thermometer) without stirring. Remove from heat. Immediately beat egg whites until stiff. Slowly pour hot syrup into beaten whites, beating at high speed for about 5 minutes. Stir in vanilla; beat until mixture forms soft peaks and begins to lose its gloss. Add pecans, if desired. Drop by teaspoonful onto waxed paper. If divinity becomes too stiff, add a few drops of hot water.

Makes 1½ pounds.

Judy Mitchell

▪ *Aunt Bill's Brown Candy* ▪

When I asked my Aunt Tip for some of her favorite recipes, she said right off, "Do you have Aunt Bill's Brown Candy?" She said that this is an old candy recipe that probably every cook in Oklahoma and North Texas prepared during the 1940's for any special occasion. It seems that Aunt Bill was a radio personality or newspaper writer in Oklahoma City, and she gave this recipe via radio or newspaper. Over and over this recipe would have to be repeated, since people would write in and ask for it again and again. Everyone who eats it swears it is one of the best candy recipes, so for future generations, here is the famous Aunt Bill's Brown Candy.

6 cups sugar, divided
2 cups whole milk (or use cream,
　which is even better)
¼ teaspoon baking soda
1 stick butter
1 teaspoon vanilla
2 cups pecans

Melt 2 cups of sugar in heavy skillet (cast-iron works well). As soon as the sugar starts to heat pour the remaining 4 cups sugar and the milk into a deep stainless kettle and let it cook slowly over low heat. As soon as the sugar in skillet is melted, begin pouring it into the kettle of boiling milk and sugar, keeping it on a very low heat and stirring constantly. Cook until it forms a soft ball when dropped in cold water. Remove from heat and immediately add soda, stirring vigorously. Add butter; stir and allow to melt. Cool for 20 minutes (you should be able to touch the pan bottom). Add vanilla and pecans and begin beating until candy turns dull and becomes thick. Pour into buttered pan. Cool and cut into squares.

Makes 1½ pounds.

Wildred Patton

▪ *Whiskey Balls* ▪

2¼ cups vanilla wafer crumbs
1 cup finely chopped pecans
½ cup Jack Daniel's Whiskey
1 cup confectioners' sugar
3 tablespoons cocoa
2 tablespoons light corn syrup
Confectioners' sugar
Chopped pecans

Combine vanilla wafer crumbs and pecans. Place next 4 ingredients in bowl. Beat thoroughly with rotary beater or electric blender. Pour over crumb mixture; blend well. Roll into balls, then roll balls in confectioners' sugar and chopped nuts.
Makes 40 to 48 balls.

Terry Ann Noblitt

▪ *Granny Taylor's Caramel Candy* ▪

1⅔ cups (scant) caramelized sugar
Butter
½ cup milk
4 cups sugar
1 13-ounce can evaporated milk
⅛ teaspoon salt
⅛ teaspoon baking soda
1 stick butter (not margarine)
1 teaspoon vanilla
1 cup chopped pecans, optional

To caramelize sugar, put a scant 1⅔ cups sugar in an iron skillet. Turn burner on medium-high to caramelize. Sugar will melt. When melted, remove from heat. Grease saucepan with butter. Combine in saucepan milk, 4 cups sugar and evaporated milk. Heat to a rolling boil. Add evaporated milk mixture to carmelized sugar in a small stream, stirring constantly. Reduce heat to medium. Boil mixture to hard-ball stage. Remove from heat. Add salt, soda, butter and vanilla and nuts, if desired. Place pan in cool water; stir occasionally until it begins to thicken. Drop by spoonsful onto waxed paper.
Makes 3 dozen pieces.

Fran Houser

▪ *Buckeyes* ▪

These look just like the buckeyes from the farm. The trick is to make them about the size of a large marble so they are bite-size. The paraffin hardens the chocolate so they store well at room temperature. Great for party snacks and Christmas, especially if you love peanut butter.

1½ pounds confectioners' sugar, sifted
2 sticks margarine, softened
1 pound smooth peanut butter
⅓ slab paraffin, grated
½ 12-ounce package bittersweet chocolate chip morsels

Combine first 3 ingredients. Form into small balls. Chill overnight. Melt paraffin and chocolate in top of double boiler. Remove a few balls from refrigerator (they have to be cold) at a time. Insert toothpick (or knitting needle) and dip into chocolate. Place on waxed paper. Close toothpick holes with finger. Leave space around the toothpick the size of a dime so it will look like a real buckeye. Store in tightly covered container.
Makes about 125.

Renate Stone

152

Shops on the Square in Lynchburg are as varied as they are plentiful. Gene Limbaugh, president of the Chamber of Commerce, runs The Emporium, which is filled to the rafters with gifts galore. Hattie's Christmas Haus has enough ornaments, Santas, and angels to keep Christmas alive every day of the year. The Barrel Shop has souvenirs and a slew of items for home and garden made from Jack Daniel barrels. Sully's Collectibles has porcelain figurines, china dolls, and souvenirs. The Pepsi Parlor has one of the country's most complete collections of Pepsi memorabilia.

Our Place, A General Store carries a variety of plates, figurines and carvings for serious collectors. They ship orders for limited editions daily. The Soda Shop serves dozens of flavors of ice cream cones, sundaes, or sodas — a great break for any shopper. Mary Ruth Fuqua's Antiques is for the serious antique shopper.

The Lynchburg Hardware and General Store has everything from green salve to a wooden coffin, but tee shirts and Jack Daniel items are the best sellers. At the Pepper Patch you can watch them hand-dip chocolate Tennessee Truffles or bake a Tennessee Tipsy Cake, but the best part is sampling some fruit butters or sherried pecans.

Wander in and say hi to the folks at the Farmer's Bank, the Drug Store, *The Moore County News*, and the Farmers' Co-op. They are all happy to greet visitors to their hometown. Buy a Goo Goo at the Lynchburg Grocery or a whiskey burger at The Iron Kettle before you go. Sit on a courthouse bench and whittle or just snap pictures of some of the farmers selling produce from their trucks.

Best of all, visit us during one of our special celebrations: Frontier Days, International Barbecue Cookoff, or Christmas in the Hollow. Or choose a local event such as a horse show, tractor pull, or stock auction. We think you will enjoy your visit, so come see us!

▪ *Neiman's $250 Cookie Recipe* ▪

The following recipe has an interesting story which was featured on a television show in Nashville. A lady was eating at Neiman-Marcus in Dallas and the featured dessert was this famous chocolate chip cookie. Thinking out loud how wonderful the cookie was, she asked the waitress if the chef shared his recipe. The answer was "yes" and she left with recipe in tow. Paying for lunch with a credit card, she didn't notice until the bill came that she had been charged $250 for the recipe. She called back to protest, but all they said was "tough luck." To get back at the chef and the restaurant, she gave the recipe to one and all.

4 sticks butter
2 cups sugar
2 cups packed brown sugar
4 eggs
2 teaspoons vanilla
4 cups all-purpose flour
5 cups blended oatmeal
1 teaspoon salt
2 teaspoons baking powder
2 teaspoons baking soda
24 ounces semi-sweet chocolate morsels or white chocolate
1 8-ounce Hershey's candy bar, grated
3 cups chopped pecans or macadamia nuts

Preheat oven to 375°. Cream butter and both sugars; add eggs and vanilla. Combine flour, blended oatmeal (made by processing oatmeal to a fine powder 2 cups at a time in blender), salt, baking powder and soda. Add chocolate, grated candy bar and nuts. Roll into balls and place 2 inches apart on a cookie sheet. Bake for 6 minutes. *Note:* Recipe may be halved.

Makes 112 cookies.

▪ *Cornmeal Cookies* ▪

2 sticks butter or margarine, at room temperature
1 cup sugar
2 egg yolks
1 teaspoon grated lemon peel
1½ cups all-purpose flour
1 cup yellow cornmeal
Sugar

Place butter and 1 cup sugar in a medium mixing bowl; beat with an electric mixer until lighter in color and well blended. Add egg yolks; mix well. Stir in lemon peel, flour and cornmeal until well mixed. Wrap dough in a plastic bag; chill for 3 to 4 hours or until firm. Preheat oven to 350°. Roll the dough out on a very lightly floured surface or between sheets of waxed paper to a ¼-inch thickness. Cut into heart shapes using a 2½-inch cutter. Place on an ungreased baking sheet; sprinkle with additional sugar. Bake in center of oven for about 8 to 10 minutes or until edges are browned. *Note:* Dough may be rolled into a 2-inch cylinder before chilling and cut into rounds about ¼-inch thick before baking.

Makes 3 dozen cookies.

Norma Rigler

▪ *The Ultimate Chocolate Chip Cookie* ▪

2 sticks unsalted butter, cut into chunks
1 cup packed brown sugar
¾ cup granulated sugar
1 teaspoon salt, optional
2 large eggs
1½ teaspoons vanilla
2½ cups all-purpose flour
1¼ teaspoons baking soda
2 cups walnuts, coarsely chopped
3 cups semi-sweet chocolate morsels

In a large bowl, beat butter, sugars, and salt with an electric mixer until creamy and no butter flecks remain. Beat in eggs and vanilla until well blended. Add flour and baking soda; beat until well blended. With a spoon, stir in walnuts and chocolate morsels.

With a small ice cream scoop or ¼-cup measure (fill cup about half full), shape dough into 1½-inch-diameter balls (about 2½ tablespoons). Place close together on 10x15-inch baking sheets. Cover and chill at least 6 hours or up to 4 days. (If time is short, you can omit chilling step, but cookies may not brown as rapidly.)

To bake, transfer cookie balls to 12x15-inch baking sheets, ungreased or lined with cooking parchment; space balls about 2½ inches apart. Flatten each ball to a ¾ inch-thick round; make sides go straight up and depress center of each cookie slightly. Let cookie dough warm to room temperature, about 30 minutes. Preheat oven to 400°.

Bake for 8 to 10 minutes or until cookies are golden brown all around edges but center 1 inch is still pale. (If you bake 2 pans in 1 oven, switch pan positions halfway through baking for more even browning.) Remove from oven and cool on pans until firm, about 5 minutes. Transfer to wire racks. Serve cookies warm or cool.

If made more than 1 day ahead, cool, cover and freeze in an airtight container. To reheat, place frozen cookies slightly apart on 12x15-inch baking sheets. Bake in a 200° oven until warm, 12 to 15 minutes. *Note:* The extra flour in this recipe helps maintain a plump shape and keeps the cookie from spreading. Brief baking at a high temperature forms a crust on the outside and maintains a moist, chewy inside.

Makes 3 to 3½ dozen.

Georgia Sewell

▪ *No Cholesterol Oatmeal Cookies* ▪

½ cup granulated sugar
½ cup packed brown sugar
¼ cup vegetable oil
Egg substitute, equal to 2 eggs
2 teaspoons vanilla
1 cup sifted all-purpose flour
¼ teaspoon baking soda
1½ cups 1-minute oats, uncooked
⅓ cup pecans
⅓ cup raisins

Preheat oven to 350°. Mix sugars, oil, egg substitute and vanilla. Combine flour and soda. Blend into sugar mixture. Blend in oats, pecans and raisins. Drop by tablespoonsful onto lightly greased baking sheet. Bake for 8 to 10 minutes or until lightly browned.

Makes 3 dozen.

Sara Norman

Fried catfish and a party will bring a crowd together faster than flies to honey. The Jack Daniel Distillery draws thousands of visitors every year and some are there in time for a company party. The catfish and hush puppies, barbecue and cole slaw are typical Southern fare and the hospitality is friendly and befitting the South. The party is all-around old-fashioned fun.

■ *Oatmeal Cookies* ■

This is my favorite recipe for Oatmeal Cookies, which I learned in my Home Economics Class in high school. Mrs. Marshall was my teacher at Tullahoma High School. I made the cookies as a teenager because my family liked them and Mama had the ingredients most of the time, except the raisins. I used hickory nuts or black walnuts. Now I use pecans and use margarine in place of butter.

2 sticks butter
1 cup sugar
1 egg, well beaten
⅓ cup sour milk
1 cup chopped raisins or nuts
1½ cups all-purpose flour
⅛ teaspoon salt
½ teaspoon cinnamon
½ teaspoon baking soda
½ teaspoon baking powder
1½ cups rolled oats

Preheat oven to 350°. Cream butter; add sugar, egg and milk. Dust raisins with a small amount of flour. Sift remaining flour with salt, cinnamon, soda and baking powder. Stir in oats; add gradually to butter mixture. Add raisins. Drop by spoonsful onto greased pans or baking sheets. Bake for 15 to 20 minutes or until lightly browned.
  Makes 3 dozen.

Frances Bailey

■ *Grandma Gerrie's Butter Cookies* ■

2 sticks butter (not margarine)
5 tablespoons sugar
1 teaspoon vanilla
2 cups sifted all-purpose flour
  Pecan halves
  Sugar

Preheat oven to 350°. Cream butter; add sugar, vanilla and flour. Mix well. Form dough into balls. Place on ungreased cookie sheets. Press pecan halves into top of each cookie. Bake for 12 to 15 minutes or until light brown on bottom. Remove from oven. While still warm, roll in sugar.
  Makes 3 dozen.

Gerrie Honeycutt

156

▪ *Snickerdoodles* ▪

This cookie is delicious and it fills the house with a good cinnamon smell.

½ cup solid shortening
1 stick butter, softened
1½ cups sugar
2 eggs
2¾ cups all-purpose flour
2 teaspoons cream of tartar
1 teaspoon baking soda
¼ teaspoon salt
2 tablespoons sugar
2 teaspoons cinnamon

Preheat oven to 400°. Mix shortening, butter 1½ cups sugar and eggs thoroughly. Stir together flour, cream of tartar, soda and salt; blend into shortening mixture. Form into 1-inch balls. Roll in mixture of 2 tablespoons sugar and cinnamon. Place about 2 inches apart on ungreased baking sheet. Bake for 8 to 10 minutes. Cookies will be soft when taken from oven. Do not overbake. Makes a chewy cookie.

Makes about 6 dozen.

Bobbie Payne

▪ *Mrs. Rutledge's Sugar Cookies* ▪

This is a real old-fashioned sugar cookie that really satisfies.

1 egg
½ cup sugar
½ cup confectioners' sugar
½ cup vegetable oil
1 stick butter, softened
2¾ cups self-rising flour
½ teaspoon baking soda
½ teaspoon cream of tartar
1 teaspoon vanilla
Pecan halves

Preheat oven to 350°. Beat the egg, sugars, oil and butter until light and fluffy. Mix the dry ingredients; blend into egg mixture. Stir in vanilla. Form dough into small balls and place on an ungreased baking sheet. Flatten each ball with a fork; sprinkle with sugar. Top with a pecan, if desired. Bake for 10 to 12 minutes or until still soft in center. Remove and cool on wire rack.

Makes 5 dozen.

Mrs. Lilbern Rutledge

▪ *Fudge Bars* ▪

1 stick butter
2 squares unsweetened chocolate
2 eggs
1 cup sugar
1 teaspoon vanilla
½ cup all-purpose flour
Pinch of salt
1 cup chopped nuts

Preheat oven to 350°. Grease a 9-inch square baking pan. Melt butter and chocolate in a saucepan. Remove from heat; let cool. Meanwhile beat eggs, sugar and vanilla together. Add melted chocolate mixture; beat well. Blend in flour and salt. Stir in nuts; pour into greased pan. Bake for 25 minutes or until firm in center. Cool and cut into squares.

Makes 1 dozen.

John & Kathy Barnes

▪ *Reese's Peanut Butter Cookies* ▪

This is a great recipe for kids to enjoy eating and making. It's also a favorite at bake sales.

1 roll refrigerator peanut butter cookies
1 bag miniature Reese's peanut butter cups

Cut roll of cookies into 9 slices, then cut each slice into quarters, making 36 cookies. Roll into balls. Press balls into miniature muffin tins. Bake according to package directions. Cookies will form a tiny crust like a pie shell. As soon as the cookies come out of the oven, insert a Reese's peanut butter cup (paper removed) into center of cookie. Cool before removing from pan.
Makes 36 cookies.

Lynne Farrar

▪ *Mama Groves' Brownies* ▪

2 cups sugar
1½ cups self-rising flour
½ cup cocoa
2 sticks butter, melted
4 eggs
2 teaspoons vanilla

Preheat oven to 325°. Mix dry ingredients. Pour in melted butter and mix until all dry ingredients are wet. Add eggs, one at a time, beating slowly after each addition. Add vanilla; mix well. Pour into a greased 13x9x2-inch baking dish. Bake for 30 to 35 minutes or until still soft in the middle.
Makes 12 to 16 squares.

Judy Mitchell

▪ *Wonderful Brownies* ▪

Are you in the mood for something chocolate, nutty, chewy? Then here is the perfect thing to satisfy your craving. (Who is counting calories?)

½ cup vegetable oil
1 cup sugar
1 teaspoon vanilla
2 eggs
½ cup self-rising flour
⅓ cup cocoa
½ cup chopped pecans

Preheat oven to 350°. Blend oil, sugar and vanilla in a bowl. Add eggs; beat well with a spoon. In a separate bowl, blend flour and cocoa, then add gradually to the egg mixture until well blended. Stir in nuts. Pour into a greased 9-inch square pan. Bake for 20 to 25 minutes or until firm on sides but still soft in the middle. Cool in pan. Cut into 16 squares.
Makes 16 servings.

Renate Stone

158

▪ *Butterscotch Brownies* ▪

2 6-ounce packages butterscotch
   morsels
1 stick butter
4 eggs
1 cup packed light brown sugar
1½ cups all-purpose flour
2 cups chopped pecans

Preheat oven to 350°. Melt butterscotch morsels and butter in top of double boiler, over hot, not boiling, water. Beat eggs and sugar in bowl; sift in flour. Add butterscotch mixture. Mix well. Stir in pecans. Pour into lightly greased pan. Bake for 25 minutes or until still soft in center.

Makes 12 to 16 squares.

Bonnie Darnell

▪ *Apricot Pastries* ▪

2 cups dried apricots
2 cups water
3 cups sifted all-purpose flour
1 tablespoon sugar
½ teaspoon salt
1 cup solid shortening
½ cup milk
1 package active dry yeast
1 slightly beaten egg
½ teaspoon vanilla
   Confectioners' sugar

Simmer dried apricots in water until tender; set aside to cool. Sift together flour, sugar and salt. Cut in shortening using pastry blender or two knives until mixture resembles coarse crumbs. Scald milk; cool to warm. Add yeast and let soften. Add egg and vanilla; add to flour mixture. Mix well. Divide dough into 4 parts. On a surface well dusted with confectioners' sugar, roll out 1 part at a time to form a 10-inch square. Cut each into sixteen 2½-inch squares. Place heaping teaspoonful of apricots in center of each. Pinch 2 opposite corners together. Place 2 inches apart on greased cookie sheet. Let stand 10 minutes. Preheat oven to 350°. Bake about 10 to 12 minutes. Remove at once from pan. Roll in confectioners' sugar; cool on wire rack.

Makes 64 pastries.

Mary Edwards

▪ SPECIALTIES ▪

In restaurants it is always fun to try the specialty of the house, an outstanding dish by which the chef wants to be known. Home cooks also have specialties of their houses. They may be original recipes or old favorites embellished and improved to make them really different. A specialty could be a salad, a relish, a sauce or a condiment.

In this chapter we include two kinds of specialties. First, there are recipes that make a meal special, which seem to be more at home in a special category than anywhere else. Second, there are recipes that are better than the average. These are extra-special all-time winners. Whichever kind of specialty you try first, it will make your celebration extra special.

▪ George's Quick And Easy Batter For Fish ▪

1 cup self-rising flour
1 egg, beaten
Beer

Combine flour and egg. Add enough beer to make a smooth batter. Dip fish in batter and fry. It will have a light and crispy texture.

Makes 1 cup.

George Upchurch

161

▪ *Honeymoon Hash* ▪

When I first married in 1930, I lived in Johnson City, Tennessee in an apartment house. Mr. Hale, who ran the apartment house, was cooking this one night in his basement apartment. It smelled so good, and he gave me some of it and also his recipe.

3 large potatoes, peeled and cubed
1 pound bulk pork country
   sausage
1 large onion, chopped

Cook potatoes in lightly salted boiling water until tender. Drain. Fry sausage and onion together until done. Add cooked potatoes and brown. Drain excess grease before serving. Serve with pinto beans and cooked apples.
   Makes 6 servings.

Mary D. Holt

▪ *Hunter's Chili* ▪

A favorite luncheon meal at our house during hunting season is chili. Since I'm never sure what time my husband and his friends will arrive for lunch, I need a meal I can serve on very short notice. This recipe allows me to prepare the chili, put it on low heat to simmer, and when the hunters come in, they find a delicious hot meal waiting for them.

1 pound ground venison or beef
1 medium onion, chopped
2 16-ounce cans hot chili beans,
   undrained
1 16-ounce can tomato sauce
   Chili powder

Combine meat and onion in Dutch oven; cook until meat is browned. Drain off excess drippings. Add beans, tomato sauce and chili powder to taste. Cook over low heat; simmer until ready to eat.
   Makes 4 to 6 servings.

Peggy Gray

▪ *LaVerne's Favorite Salad Dressing* ▪

1 pint Hellman's mayonnaise
1 pint buttermilk
   Juice of ½ a lemon
1 package Good Seasons Garlic
   Salad Dressing Mix
1 package Good Seasons Italian
   Salad Dressing Mix
1 package Frito Brand Green
   Onion Salad Dressing Mix
½ teaspoon sugar
½ teaspoon salt

Combine all ingredients; blend well. Refrigerate until time to serve. Will keep well in refrigerator.
   Makes 1 quart.

LaVerne Patton

▪ *Honey French Dressing* ▪

½ cup honey
1 cup vegetable oil
½ teaspoon salt
⅓ cup chili sauce
½ cup vinegar
1 medium onion, grated
1 tablespoon Worcestershire sauce

Place all ingredients in quart jar; shake well. Chill before serving.
Makes 1 pint.

Ilene Brown

▪ *Lemon French Dressing* ▪

½ cup lemon juice
½ cup vegetable oil
1 teaspoon salt
1 teaspoon paprika
2 tablespoons sugar
½ teaspoon celery seed
1 clove garlic, grated

Place all ingredients in quart jar; shake well.
Makes 1 cup.

Ilene Brown

▪ *Vinnie Leal's Indian Relish* ▪

Last year while visiting my Aunt Tip in Chattanooga (Oklahoma, that is) we spent a wonderful evening going through her recipes. She had a number of recipes given to her by her sister-in-law, Vinnie Leal Patton, known in those parts as a wonderful friend and cook. Among these recipes we found a note which is evidence that great cooks are dear to the heart of family and friends. It said:

To Vinnie Leal:
In your sweet face, there is a trace
Of whence you came one golden hour.
You are to me, all you should be,
A gracious, unpretentious flower.

8 green tomatoes, chopped
4 large red or green sweet peppers, chopped
3 large onions, chopped
Salt to taste
1 quart apple cider vinegar
1 pound sugar
1 teaspoon mustard seed
1 teaspoon ground cinnamon
1 teaspoon ground allspice
2 teaspoons ground ginger

Combine all ingredients in a large pan. Boil for 15 minutes; pour into a sterile jar. Seal and process in boiling water bath. Cool; then refrigerate.
Makes 8 half-pint jars.

Vinnie Leal Patton

163

▪ *Crab and Corn Cakes with Jack Daniel's Whiskey Butter* ▪

3 cups fresh corn—cut off the cob
3 whole eggs
2 egg yolks
½ cup all-purpose flour
½ cup yellow cornmeal
3 tablespoons clarified butter
  Salt and pepper to taste
¼ pound fresh lump crab meat, shredded
¼ cup chopped chives
  Jack Daniel's Whiskey Butter
  (recipe follows)

Using a food processor, pureé the corn to a slightly coarse texture. Stir in remaining ingredients and mix thoroughly. Using a 1-ounce ladle of batter for each cake, fry the cakes on a hot, greased griddle until brown on each side. Serve with Jack Daniel's Whiskey butter.
  Makes about 16 cakes.

Jack Daniel's Whiskey Butter

½ stick butter, softened
½ teaspoon dry mustard
2 teaspoons wine vinegar
2 teaspoons Worcestershire sauce
¼ teaspoon salt
  Dash of cayenne pepper
2 egg yolks
3 tablespoons Jack Daniel's Whiskey

Combine all ingredients well. Spoon into small crock or dish. Chill to harden.

▪ *Spiked Cranberry Relish* ▪

I used to prepare this relish just during the Christmas holidays, but my husband has such a fit over it that he insists that I keep it in the refrigerator year-round. (I freeze bags of fresh cranberries during December to use later in the year.) It is delicious and can accompany a ham sandwich for a light supper.

4 cups (1 pound) cranberries
1 whole orange, seeds removed, and quartered
2 cups sugar
¼ cup Jack Daniel's Whiskey

Using food processor, chop cranberries and orange. Add sugar; chop again to combine. Place in covered container. Chill for 24 hours. Add Jack Daniel's Whiskey just before serving. (The color is so pretty—serve in a glass compote.)
  Makes 1 quart.

Mary Jane Boyd

Competitions and Contests

Barbara Wright

Competitions can be fun or frustrating. However, Barbara Wright enjoys competition, and so she enters everything from shooting matches to cooking contests. And she always places well.

If there is one person in Lynchburg that exemplifies all the complexities of the modern-day woman, it would be Barbara Wright. She is a woman of many accomplishments. As human resource coordinator at the Jack Daniel Distillery, she can keep you abreast of all the "happnin's in de holler," and she even edits a newsletter by that name. This in itself is a full-time endeavor, but she also finds time to do many other things.

She likes to write poetry and has had a number of poems published. She loves to fish and can hold her own with the best of fishermen. A skilled marksman, she loves to hunt and enjoys competitive shooting, both professional competitions and local ones with the security guards at the distillery. Her marks are high and she places well.

Barbara comes from a long line of good cooks, including her dad, now 75 years old. He can whip up a great meal, but his specialties are cakes and pies. Barbara's favorite is his tickle-your-tastebuds angel food cake.

Last year Barbara entered a competition for recipes using Bols liqueur in the ingredients. She "conjured up" (her own words) a special applesauce recipe and is shown here with her presentation for the judges in Louisville. It won her two ribbons and some nice prizes —proof that food and celebrations go hand in hand.

▪ *Sugar And Spice Pecans* ▪

¾ cup sugar
1 egg white
2½ tablespoons water
1 teaspoon ground cinnamon
½ teaspoon salt
¼ teaspoon allspice
¼ teaspoon ground cloves
8 cups pecan halves

Preheat oven to 275°. Combine first 7 ingredients in a large bowl; mix well. Add pecans; stir until evenly coated. Spread pecans onto a greased 15x10x1-inch jelly-roll pan. Bake for 50 to 55 minutes. Remove to waxed paper while still warm. Cool. Store in an airtight container.
Makes 8 cups.

Bonnie Darnell

▪ *Angel Food Cake Topping* ▪

This is my grandmother Edde's very old recipe. It was served on angel food cake or on plain cake and ice cream. Quick and so good!

1 cup sugar
½ cup buttermilk
1 stick margarine, melted
½ teaspoon baking soda
1 teaspoon vanilla
1 tablespoon white corn syrup

Combine all ingredients in saucepan. Bring to a rapid boil for 1 minute. Serve immediately.
Makes 1 cup.

Sandra Bedford

▪ *Hard Sauce* ▪

1 stick butter, softened
3 cups sugar
Pinch of salt
⅓ cup Jack Daniel's Whiskey

Cream butter and gradually beat in sugar until creamy and light and sugar has dissolved. Beat in salt and Jack Daniel's Whiskey. Delicious over prune cake or pound cake.
Makes 2 cups.

▪ *Jezebel Sauce* ▪

This is a great "gift from the kitchen" when put in half-pint jars.

1 12-ounce jar apple jelly
1 12-ounce jar pineapple preserves
1 5-ounce bottle horseradish
1 1½-ounce can dry mustard

Blend all ingredients thoroughly. Refrigerate. Serve with meats. This will keep in refrigerator for 6 to 8 weeks.
Makes 3 cups.

▪ *Blackberry Jam* ▪

4 cups (about 2 quarts) crushed,
   fully ripe blackberries
7 cups (3 pounds) sugar
3 ounces liquid fruit pectin
8 to 10 half-pint jars with lids,
   sterilized and drained

In large saucepan, combine berries and sugar. Bring to a full rolling boil over high heat; boil hard for 1 minute, stirring constantly. Remove from heat and stir in pectin. With metal spoon, skim off foam. Alternately skim and stir for about 5 minutes to cool slightly. Fill prepared jelly jars to within ½-inch of top. With clean, damp cloth, wipe away any spills from containers. Seal and process in boiling water bath for 10 minutes. Allow jars to cool overnight, away from drafts, before storing.

Makes about 8 cups.

Barbara McGear

▪ *Tipsy Cranberries* ▪

This recipe dates back to 1740 using apple brandy. But in Lynchburg, we like to substitute our hometown product instead of the brandy.

2 cups fresh cranberries
2 cups sugar
¼ cup apple brandy or Jack
   Daniel's Whiskey

Preheat oven to 300°. Wash the cranberries well, and spread them evenly on the bottom of a greased, shallow baking dish with a cover. Sprinkle sugar evenly over the cranberries. Cover; bake for 1 hour, stirring the cranberries occasionally. When done, remove the cover, and pour the apple brandy or Jack Daniel's Whiskey over all. Stir gently.

Makes 6 to 8 servings.

Artie Mae Renegar

▪ *Brandied Apple Sauce* ▪

This recipe won creative cook Barbara Wright two ribbons in the Best of Bols liqueur contest in Louisville. The first was a ribbon for third best in its category and the second was a third overall. Serve hot or cold. This is excellent with pork chops, chicken or potato pancakes!

6 tart green apples
2 cups water
1 cup confectioners' sugar
1 teaspoon ground cinnamon
½ cup Bols Fruit Flavored Brandy
   of choice (Apricot, Peach,
   Blackberry, etc.)

Peel, core and quarter the apples. Place in water. Cook over low heat until apples soften; stir occasionally. Remove from heat; drain and add sugar, cinnamon and brandy. Simmer 5 minutes . . . and enjoy!

Makes 1 quart.

Barbara Wright

■ BARBECUE ■

There is nothing that celebrates summer like an old-fashioned cookout! Stack the charcoal, stoke up the fire, pat out the meat for burgers, and roast a weiner on a coat hanger—summer is here when you smell the sweet smoke of charcoal from the neighbor's backyard. Shrimp skewered on the grill, roasted ears of fresh corn, barbecued ribs or pork shoulder smoked over hickory or sugar maple coals are all part of the great American pastime every summer.

Dishes that go along with cookouts are homemade ice cream and cobbler, potato salad or slaw, watermelon, pickles, and relishes. All these good things add to the specialness of a cookout.

Barbecuing is the easy way to entertain, with everyone joining both in the work and in the fun. Light the fire and try some of these new dishes at your next cookout.

■ *Barbecued Ribs* ■

2 pounds pork ribs
  Adolph's seasoned meat
    tenderizer
12 to 14 ounces tomato catsup
½ cup white vinegar
½ cup packed light brown sugar
½ cup grated onion
½ teaspoon red pepper flakes or
    more
  Dash of salt

Cut ribs into serving pieces. Sprinkle ribs with meat tenderizer. Place in stockpot with enough water to cover. Cover and cook until tender. Combine remaining ingredients in saucepan. Bring to a boil. Reduce heat and simmer for 15 minutes. Preheat oven to 350°. Place ribs in baking dish; pour sauce over ribs. Bake for 30 minutes.
  Makes 4 servings.
    Served at Miss Mary Bobo's Boarding House

169

▪ *Gray's Barbecue Sauce* ▪

Every year our family gathers on July 4th for fireworks, pool-playtime and the best food in the Southeast. The festivities begin July 3rd with the traditional "digging of the pit." In an out-of-the-way place in the backyard a 1½- to 2-foot pit is dug and lined with bricks. Around midnight, a wire grill is stretched over the coals and 1 to 2 pork shoulders are slapped on. The entire pit is then covered with dampened, torn cardboard boxes. All family members are invited to sleep over and are encouraged to volunteer for a "pit watch." A half-and-half mixture of vinegar and lemon juice is brushed on the shoulders every hour. Our menu includes: Pork shoulders, barbecue chicken, grilled lobsters, cole slaw, baked beans, deviled eggs, roast corn on the cob, iced tea with fresh mint, homemade ice cream and cold watermelons. We also have a special barbecue sauce in which we dip the cooked, pulled meat.

¼ cup packed brown sugar
¼ cup prepared mustard
¼ cup cider vinegar
1 tablespoon soy sauce
⅛ teaspoon red pepper
½ teaspoon garlic salt
½ teaspoon onion salt
¾ cup catsup

Combine all ingredients in saucepan. Simmer 30 minutes to 1 hour or until thickened. *Note:* Don't brush sauce on while cooking meat, or it will burn. Use before serving.
Makes 1½ cups.

Dr. Bob Gray

▪ *Phoenix Brand World Championship Barbecue Sauce* ▪

This is the Holy Smoker's Competition Barbecue team's sauce recipe. Keith Bennett was the winner of the sauce category at the First Annual Jack Daniel's Barbecue Cook-off held in Lynchburg in October, 1989.

½ large onion, minced
4 cloves garlic, minced
¾ cup Jack Daniel's Whiskey
2 cups catsup
⅓ cup vinegar
¼ cup Worcestershire sauce
½ cup packed brown sugar
¾ cup molasses
½ teaspoon black pepper
½ tablespoon salt
¼ cup tomato paste
2 to 3 tablespoons liquid smoke
⅓ teaspoon Tabasco, or less

Combine onion, garlic, and Jack Daniel's Whiskey in a 3-quart saucepan. Sauté until onion and garlic are translucent, approximately 10 minutes. Remove from heat and light mixture; flame for 20 seconds. Add all remaining ingredients. Bring to a boil, then turn down to a medium simmer. Simmer 20 minutes, stirring constantly. Run sauce through a medium strainer to remove onion and garlic bits if you prefer a smoother sauce. Cool and enjoy. *Note:* This sauce gets better with age. If time permits, keep it in the refrigerator a day or so to develop a deeper, richer taste.
Makes 4 cups.

Keith Bennett

• *Uncle Jack's Margarita Steak* •

6 ribeye steaks
  Salt and pepper
¼ cup olive oil
1 clove garlic, crushed
1 medium onion, chopped
1 tablespoon lime juice
1 tablespoon sugar
½ teaspoon cornstarch
1 tablespoon Jack Daniel's
  Whiskey
1 tablespoon beef stock

Season steaks with salt and pepper. In a large cast-iron skillet, heat oil to moderate temperature. Sauté garlic in oil until browned. Remove garlic; add steaks. Cook 2 to 3 minutes per side for medium rare. Remove and place on warm platter until all steaks are cooked. Add onion to skillet and cook until glazed, scraping bottom of pan to loosen any bits that might stick. Mix remaining ingredients well; pour into skillet. Cook and stir until thickened. Pour over steaks; serve immediately.

Makes 6 servings.

• *Glazed Beef Ribs* •

1 cup Jack Daniel's Whiskey
1 cup molasses
1 cup chili sauce
2 tablespoons Worcestershire
  sauce
2 tablespoons steak sauce
1 6-ounce can frozen orange juice,
  undiluted
3 racks beef ribs, cracked every 3
  inches
  Salt and pepper to taste

Mix first 6 ingredients together for glaze. Set aside. Parboil ribs for 30 to 45 minutes to render fat. Drain. Rub ribs with salt and pepper. Place on grill. Brush glaze on ribs, turning frequently to prevent charring. Cook until tender.

Makes 4 to 6 servings.

• *Marinated Smoked Chuck Roast* •

1 2-pound chuck roast, 1½ inches
  thick
4 cloves garlic, peeled
¼ cup vegetable oil
¼ cup wine vinegar
1 tablespoon Worcestershire sauce
½ teaspoon salt
½ teaspoon dried basil, crumbled
¼ teaspoon pepper
2 cups wood chips

Stud roast with garlic by inserting tip of knife in meat and pushing cloves into meat; evenly space garlic. Combine oil, vinegar, Worcestershire sauce, salt, basil and pepper. Place meat in plastic bag; add marinade. Set in shallow baking dish, marinate overnight in refrigerator. Soak wood chips in water for 30 minutes, drain chips. Prepare fire. When coals have grayed over, arrange around drip pan for indirect method and add 1 cup chips to coals. Drain meat, reserving marinade. Place roast on grid over drip pan. Grill roast; add 1 cup chips to fire and grill an additional 20 minutes for medium. Remove garlic before serving.

Makes 6 servings.

▪ *Hickory Smoked Ribs* ▪

4 to 6 pounds spareribs or baby-
  back ribs
1 tablespoon celery salt
1 teaspoon garlic powder
1 tablespoon chili powder
1 tablespoon brown sugar
  Barbecue sauce
2 cups wood chips

Remove membrane on back of ribs. Combine celery salt, garlic powder, chili powder and brown sugar; rub mixture over ribs. Soak wood chips in water for 30 minutes. Drain chips. Prepare fire. When coals have grayed over, arrange around drip pan for indirect method and add 1 cup chips to coals. Place ribs in smoker or on grill. Smoke ribs 3 to 4 hours. Add additional chips as needed. During the last hour of cooking time, brush occasionally with barbecue sauce.

Makes 4 to 6 servings.

▪ *Spareribs Delicious* ▪

3 pounds spareribs, cracked in 3-
  inch lengths
2½ to 3 teaspoons Kitchen Bouquet
3 tablespoons vegetable oil
  Salt and pepper
¼ cup undiluted frozen orange
  juice
¼ cup catsup
¼ cup Jack Daniel's Whiskey
1 orange, sliced
1 lemon, sliced
1 large onion, sliced

Parboil ribs in water for 40 minutes to render off the fat. Drain. With pastry brush, brush both sides of ribs with Kitchen Bouquet. Brown ribs in oil on both sides. Salt and pepper generously. Combine juice, catsup and Jack Daniel's Whiskey; set aside. Preheat oven to 350°. Arrange orange, lemon and onion slices in layers on ribs. Pour sauce over all. Bake, covered, for about 2 hours until tender, basting every 15 minutes.

Makes 3 to 4 servings.

Dorothy Overstreet

▪ *Barbecue Pot Roast* ▪

1 4 to 5-pound chuck roast
5 cloves garlic, chopped
  Salt and pepper to taste
1 cup Jack Daniel's Whiskey
¼ cup oregano, or less
¾ cup olive oil
¼ cup chopped parsley
  Juice of 3 lemons
1 cup catsup

On large sheet of foil, place roast in center (shiny-side of foil up). Make slits in roast and insert pieces of garlic into slits. Salt and pepper generously. Mix all other ingredients, except catsup. Place roast into shallow baking pan. Push coals to one end of the grill. Place roasting pan at other end. Pour half of basting sauce over roast. Make a loose tent with foil over roast, but leave end away from fire open so smoke can penetrate the meat. After an hour mix catsup with remaining sauce. Open grill and lift foil; pour remaining sauce over meat and remove foil. Close grill and continue to cook for another hour.

Makes 6 to 8 servings.

Barbecues

Frank Bobo

Bobo is a well-known name in these parts, but Frank Bobo is a man known in other parts of the world as well as the master distiller at Jack Daniel's.

Soon after Frank returned home from the Korean War, Reagor Motlow, son of Lem Motlow who owned the Jack Daniel Distillery, came by Frank's father's grocery store and asked young Frank if he would like to work for him. The grocery made a good living for two families (Frank's dad and brother), but with Frank back from the service, three families for one grocery in Lynchburg seemed a stretch. Frank took Mr. Reagor up on the offer.

Under the tutorship of Lem Tolley, Frank learned all about the distilling business. He became master distiller when Mr. Lem retired. As the Jack Daniel name became better known, the master distiller's fame also grew. Over the years Frank has met thousands of visitors to the distillery. He has had his picture taken by many and had his name mentioned in many news stories.

Frank is a sportsman and excels in golfing, fishing, and hunting. He is also an avid outdoor cook. For many years he has prepared barbecue for company parties and picnics and he continues doing this for his family get-togethers. His wife, Ava Lee, their daughters, and their families enjoy these occasions often.

Last year Frank was official host for the Jack Daniel World Championship International Barbecue in Lynchburg. The cookoff, an invitational tournament to champions of other cookoffs, drew guests and participants from all over. Other events included an antique show, hot air balloon rides, pig racing, a greased pig chase, and street dances. Celebrities, food editors, and assorted barbecue experts came for the festivities. Frank was there greeting one and all and sharing some of his secrets for good barbecue. The cookoff was such a big success that it is to be held annually the last weekend in October.

This is a hometown celebration where spirits are high, prizes are grand, and the barbecue is the finest. Join us next year and judge for yourself!

▪ *Busy Day Brisket* ▪

My family from Texas sent this recipe. It is the perfect way to cook a brisket ahead of the party and then serve when the guests arrive.

1 8 to 10-pound brisket
¼ cup Jack Daniel's Whiskey
1 tablespoon molasses
¼ cup soy sauce
1 teaspoon peppercorns
1 tablespoon salt
4 cloves garlic, minced
2 onions, minced fine
2 stalks celery, minced

Place all ingredients, except brisket, in food processor (this will mince vegetables) and pureé. Place brisket in large zipper-type bag or wrap carefully in heavy-duty foil. Pour in marinade and seal. Leave in refrigerator for 24 hours. Next evening, remove brisket from bag and place on heavy-duty foil. Cover meat with coarsely ground pepper. Pour marinade over meat and seal again. Place well-sealed meat in an open roaster pan in a 200° oven. Bake for 8 hours or overnight. Remove from oven and rewrap meat in a clean sheet of foil, reserving any juice for serving. Slice thinly and serve hot or cold . . . delicious!

▪ *Bobo-que Ribs* ▪

1 rack of ribs
1 stick butter
1 onion, finely chopped
2 cloves garlic, minced
1 cup packed brown sugar
½ cup vinegar
2 cups orange juice (can use pineapple)
2 tablespoons soy sauce
1 teaspoon ginger
1 8-ounce can tomato sauce
Dash hot sauce

Combine all ingredients, except ribs, in a saucepan and bring to a boil. Remove from heat. On prepared coals, place rack of ribs that have been generously salted. Baste with sauce on both sides. Every 20 minutes, baste ribs and turn. Ribs will be done in 4 hours. Test by using your barbecue tongs—lift one end in a twist. Meat will bend almost double without breaking in two. Cooker can be opened or closed at intervals. When closed, the smoke flavor will be more intense.

▪ *Barbecued Sausage (or Weiners)* ▪

2 cups catsup
1 cup flat beer
¼ cup cider vinegar
¼ cup Worcestershire sauce
1 onion, chopped fine
1 tablespoon celery seed
1 clove garlic, minced
1 teaspoon dry mustard
¼ cup sugar
1 teaspoon chili powder

Mix all ingredients. Cut Kielbasa, German or Polish sausage (or any good large cased sausage) in diagonal slices about 2 inches long. (If using weiners, do not cut into pieces). Place sausage or weiners in pan with sauce and place on grill. Allow to cook until about 2 minutes before serving. Remove sausage or weiners to grid and brown slightly. Serve with buns and extra sauce.

Makes enough sauce for 8 servings.

The park in Lynchburg is the site for a lot of fun doings. There are horse shows and tractor pulls, ball games and mule sales, bazaars and flea markets. Whatever the occasion, food is always a big part of the event and people line up fast to sample the fare.

■ *Smoked Wild Boar* ■

Before you ever get started on this recipe, you must, of course, have a 4 to 5-pound shank or roast of wild boar. Since I hunt I don't have too much problem arranging to have one on hand when we get ready to cook. However, there are not too many stores in this neck-of-the-woods that carry wild boar, so I recommend that you, also, hunt your own. Hunting for boar has been likened to hunting a wife. The woods are full of them, but it is getting one you can handle that's the trick. They're nervous little critters and don't take too much to any messing around. Your best bet is to let them know that you mean business before they let you have the business. In other words, take aim and fire! With that taken care of you can move right along to the next step—that of cleaning and dressing. If you're not too good at that, then I recommend a professional do the job. Once this is accomplished, you are on your way to a delectable and succulent feast. This really is mouth-watering good. In fact, I dare say it is the best meat you will ever eat!

1 4 to 5-pound shank or roast of
   wild boar
Salt and pepper
A-1 Sauce

Generously salt and pepper a 4 to 5-pound shank or roast of wild boar meat. Add a dash of A-1 Sauce (the A-1 touch will add so much!). Carefully wrap in aluminum foil and place in a smoker grill. Cook for 4 to 5 hours making sure that the fire never flames up. Coals should be low, but consistently hot during cooking time. Add coals if necessary, so meat is completely done.

Bill Edde

175

▪ *Our Favorite Oven-Barbecued Pork* ▪

3 pounds pork chops, pork loin or
  lamb breast
1 teaspoon salt
¼ teaspoon cracked black pepper
3 large oranges
½ cup chili sauce
2 tablespoons honey
1 teaspoon Worcestershire sauce
1 large onion

Preheat oven to 325°. Layer meat in Dutch oven or roast-ing pan; sprinkle with salt and pepper. Squeeze juice from 1 orange (at least ¼ cup juice), then grate peel. In a small bowl, mix juice, peel, chili sauce, honey and Worcestershire sauce; stir to combine well. Pour sauce over meat to cover. Slice onion and place slices on top of meat. Bake for 2½ to 3 hours or until fork tender, basting occasionally. While meat is roasting, slice remaining oranges and place on meat during the last 30 minutes.

Makes 6 servings.

▪ *Broiled Lamb Chops With Fresh Rosemary* ▪

The secret to this recipe is to have fresh rosemary on hand. The chops should be lean loin. Have the butcher cut them ¾ to 1-inch thick!

Loin lamb chops (2 per person)
1 bunch fresh rosemary sprigs
  White thread cut in 15-inch
  pieces
  Olive oil
  Salt and pepper to taste

Take lamb chops and place two or three rosemary sprigs on top of each. Next take one piece of string and wrap around each chop to secure the rosemary, ending with knot on the back side. This is a little tedious, but well worth the trouble! Brush a little olive oil over each chop. Sprinkle with salt and pepper. Broil on the grill. Cook 10 minutes per side for 1-inch thick chops. Rosemary will be brown and crunchy. Wonderful in taste, but do not eat the woody center stem!

Amy Blake

▪ *Whiskey-Glazed Lamb Brochettes* ▪

Lamb (rack or loins)
  Salt and pepper to taste
1 pound sugar
1 quart red wine vinegar
5 quarts lamb or chicken stock
4 bunches fresh rosemary
½ cup Jack Daniel's Whiskey

Use rack of lamb or lamb loins, debone meat and use bones to make a rich lamb stock. Cut meat into 5-ounce medallions; place on skewers to grill. Season with salt and pepper. Boil sugar and vinegar. Add lamb stock and rosemary; cook until thick and sugar has dissolved. Add Jack Daniel's Whiskey and seasonings; strain. Brush lamb with glaze as it is being grilled.

▪ *Skewered Shrimp* ▪

6 boneless chicken breasts, flattened
9 slices smoked bacon
1 pound uncooked medium shrimp, shelled and cleaned
Sauce (recipe follows)

Cut chicken breasts into 1x3-inch strips. Place a half slice of bacon on each strip. Place a shrimp on end of strips and roll up; secure with wet bamboo skewers. Marinate in Sauce for at least 2 hours in refrigerator. Cook over coals on grill for approximately 9 minutes on each side, basting with remaining sauce.

Makes 6 to 8 servings.

Sauce

2 sticks butter
3 tablespoons water
1 pint vinegar
1 6-ounce jar prepared mustard
½ cup honey
1 6-ounce bottle Worcestershire sauce
1 clove garlic, crushed

Melt butter; combine with remaining ingredients. Mix well. After marinating, reserve sauce to baste shrimp while grilling.

▪ *Jack Daniel's Smoked Chicken* ▪

4 chicken breasts, skinned and boned
1 cup Jack Daniel's Whiskey
½ cup dried herbs de provence
Black pepper to taste

Marinate chicken breasts for 1 hour in Jack Daniel's Whiskey. Place in smoker with herbs and pepper; smoke lightly until done. Chill and slice on the bias to serve.

Makes 4 servings.

▪ *Smoked Turkey* ▪

1 12-pound turkey, fresh or thawed
1 teaspoon salt
¼ teaspoon pepper
1 rib celery, cut into 1-inch pieces
1 carrot, cut into 1-inch pieces
2 small onions, quartered
2 cups wood chips, soaked

About 8 to 10 hours before serving: Sprinkle turkey inside and out with salt and pepper, stuff with celery, carrot and onion. Insert a meat thermometer in the thigh, with the tip away from the bone. Heap about 5 pounds charcoal briquettes to one side of grill and start the fire. Wait until the coals turn gray, drain wood chips and add to the coals. Put the cooking grid in place and place turkey on grid opposite coals. Smoke-cook about 8 to 10 hours or until meat thermometer reaches 180°. Add additional charcoal and chips as needed.
Makes 12 to 15 servings.

▪ *Cowboy Beans* ▪

There were four brothers in my family who loved western movies. Mother came up with Cowboy Beans to get us to eat some vegetables when we had hamburgers and barbecue.

1 teaspoon minced garlic
1 cup chopped onion
1 cup chopped celery
1 cup chopped green pepper
1 tablespoon vegetable oil
½ cup tomato sauce
½ cup barbecue sauce
2 cups cooked white beans
2 cups cooked red kidney beans
2 cups cooked long grain rice
    Hot pepper sauce to taste

Cook garlic, onion, celery and pepper in oil until soft. Add remaining ingredients; heat thoroughly.
Makes 12 servings.

Charles & Missy Haigh

▪ *Potato Salad* ▪

This is a favorite potato salad for the Rutledge family. Mrs. Rutledge has been serving it for years and it is still favored at their get-togethers.

8 medium potatoes, boiled with
    their jackets on
2 medium onions, chopped
½ cup chopped celery
4 hard-boiled eggs, chopped
4 medium-size dill pickles,
    coarsely chopped
    Salt and pepper to taste
    Salad dressing or mayonnaise

After potatoes have cooled, cut into chunks and add remaining ingredients using enough salad dressing to make it moist. Add a little of the dill pickle juice to flavor, if desired. Chill until serving time.
Makes 10 to 12 servings.

Mrs. Lilburn Rutledge

■ *Make-Ahead Coleslaw* ■

1 large head cabbage, shredded
1 large carrot, shredded
2 stalks celery, chopped
1 medium onion, chopped
1 green pepper, chopped
1 cup apple cider vinegar
1 cup vegetable oil
1 teaspoon dry mustard
1 teaspoon celery seed
2 cups sugar
  Salt and pepper

Toss vegetables together; set aside. In a saucepan, bring the vinegar, oil, mustard and celery seed to a boil. Add sugar; stir to dissolve. Pour hot mixture over vegetables; stir to mix and salt and pepper to taste. Set slaw aside for 3 hours. Cover and chill overnight. This will keep for several days in refrigerator.

Makes 8 to 10 servings.

■ *Mom's Coleslaw* ■

Here is a very good coleslaw that my family enjoys. Over the years I have tried a lot of different dressings on slaw, but I keep going back to this one. It was my mother-in-law's recipe. She fixed it for all her family gatherings and it was a favorite then . . . it still is.

1 small cabbage, shredded
2 carrots, grated
1 onion, chopped
1½ teaspoons caraway seed
2 tablespoons sugar
1½ cups mayonnaise
½ cup vinegar
  Salt and pepper to taste

Place vegetables in a bowl and toss to mix well. Add all remaining ingredients; mix very well. Cover and chill for at least 3 hours.

Makes 12 servings.

■ *Cookout Slaw* ■

3 hard-boiled eggs
⅓ cup evaporated milk
3 tablespoons vegetable oil
1 tablespoon sugar
1½ teaspoons salt
¾ teaspoon dry mustard
  Pepper to taste
3 tablespoons vinegar
4 cups shredded cabbage
1 cup shredded carrots
1 onion, minced
1 2-ounce jar minced pimientos
½ teaspoon celery seed, optional

Slice eggs and separate the yolk and whites. In small bowl, mash egg yolk with fork. Add milk, oil, sugar, salt, mustard and pepper. Mix well. Add vinegar and stir. Chill dressing. Combine cabbage, carrots, onion, pimiento and celery seed. Chop egg whites; toss with vegetables. When ready to serve, pour dressing over all and toss well.

Makes 8 to 10 servings.

▪ *Sautéed Mushrooms* ▪

This is a wonderful side dish to grilled foods or to spoon over grilled steak for a gourmet presentation.

1 stick butter
Enough mushrooms to fill ¾ of a
medium skillet, sliced
2 medium onions, chopped
4 cloves garlic, minced
1 teaspoon chervil
Salt and pepper
1 cup water
1 tablespoon Kitchen Bouquet

Melt butter in pan. Slice mushrooms. Sauté onion and garlic for about 5 minutes. Add mushrooms, chervil, salt and pepper to taste. Cook about 10 minutes on medium heat. Stir well. Add one cup water; bring to a slow boil. Stir frequently; cook until sauce is gooey. Stir in Kitchen Bouquet. *Note:* If you want a thick sauce quickly, stir one teaspoon cornstarch or flour into ½ cup cold water; add to mushrooms. Stir constantly until thick.
Makes 4 servings.

Walt Wood

▪ *Spiced Pickled Beets* ▪

A large jar of pickled and spiced beets is always in my refrigerator—just like pickles. They have a special root flavor that is especially appealing. At all of our family gatherings, the little ones look forward to "red pickles" as they call them, and the large jar quickly disappears. I make more the following day to replace our supply. They are a good accompaniment to any meal—but are especially good on picnics and cookouts.

½ cup vinegar
1 cup sugar
1 cup beet juice
1 teaspoon whole cloves
1 teaspoon whole allspice
1 cinnamon stick
2 17-ounce cans chunk-cut beets
or whole baby beets

Combine all ingredients, except beets, in medium saucepan; stir to blend. Cook over medium heat to dissolve sugar. Add beets; simmer for 10 minutes. Pour into a clean, sterile jar. Cool; then refrigerate. Wait 1 day before serving for beets to "pickle."
Makes 2½ cups.

▪ *Jack Daniel's Braised Onions* ▪

1 tablespoon butter
1¼ pounds large Spanish onions,
peeled and thinly sliced
¼ cup Jack Daniel's Whiskey
Salt and pepper

In saucepan or skillet, melt butter over moderate heat. Reduce heat; add onions and cook slowly for 30 minutes. Add Jack Daniel's Whiskey, salt and pepper to taste. Cook until mixture is dry.
Makes 8 servings.

Jack Daniel's Welcome Center

Roger Breshears

Not many small towns can boast that they play host to more than 250,000 visitors each year — especially towns with less than 400 people. But Lynchburg can! That these visitors feel welcome can be credited to the work of Roger Brashears, who heads the Welcome Center for the Jack Daniel Distillery.

Roger is a man of many talents and sparkling wit, as demonstrated by his stories, which seem to be as prolific as the trees on the hills. Roger and his staff have been known to welcome well over a thousand visitors on a given day, take them on a tour of the distillery, treat them to a glass of lemonade, and sometimes even host them again that evening for an old-fashioned catfish fry and barbecue. His talented guides can pick up guitars, fiddles, and banjos for some old timey bluegrass pickin' and grinnin'. They often start feet to dancing, whether it be square dancing, mountain clogging, or buck dancing.

Jack Daniel's international advertising invites readers to come to Lynchburg. And come they do! Visitors arrive from Japan, Australia, New Zealand, South America, Europe — everywhere. A fun tour by Roger's guides show visitors every step in whiskey making, including a back-door peek at the gray-colored warehouses where barrels of whiskey are stacked eight stories high to age in the cool mountain air.

Roger has also been known to take a convivial group of his staff to places like Boston, Washington, D.C., and even Europe to liven up a party and start toes to tapping, Tennessee style.

Roger Brashears is a big man in Lynchburg. He is well over six feet tall in his cowboy boots, but he is also big in the generous spirit of Jack Daniel's. He welcomes small groups as genuinely as big crowds. So whatever the size of your party, come see us. Roger and his staff can promise that you will have a great time while you're here in the Jack Daniel hollow!

▪ *Fried Onion Rings* ▪

In the summer, when Vidalia onions are plentiful, our favorite snack food, picnic food or appetizer for cookouts is fried onion rings. Besides tasting so good, these onion rings help the time waiting for the barbecue to go faster. The only problem is keeping up with the demand.

Onions
1 cup all-purpose flour
   McCormick's Herb Seasoning or
   Lawry's Seasoned Salt or your
   favorite brand
1 cup beer
   Milk
   Vegetable oil or shortening

Peel and slice onions at least ¼-inch thick; separate into rings. In another bowl, place flour combined with your choice of seasoning. Add beer to flour with a little milk (the batter must be real thick, so add only a little milk.) Dip onion rings into batter; shake off excess. Fry in hot oil until golden brown. Remove from oil with fork; drain on paper towels . . . serve hot.
   Makes 6 to 8 servings.

▪ *Black-Eyed Barbecue Relish* ▪

3 16-ounce cans black-eyed peas,
   drained and rinsed
2 cups cooked, diced carrots (still
   crisp)
1 green pepper, chopped
1 red onion, chopped
1 2-ounce jar chopped pimientos,
   drained
1 clove garlic, crushed
¾ cup sugar
¾ cup apple cider vinegar
½ cup vegetable oil
5 tablespoons Worcestershire
   sauce
1 10¾-ounce can condensed
   tomato soup

Prepare vegetables; combine in bowl. Combine garlic, sugar, vinegar, oil, Worcestershire sauce and soup. Stir to mix well; pour over salad vegetables and toss to mix. Cover and refrigerate for 24 hours.
   Makes 12 servings.

▪ *Barbecued Corn On The Cob* ▪

A great way to roast corn when you are cooking out.

1 ear of corn for each guest
   Butter, softened
1 bottle prepared barbecue sauce
   sauce

Shuck and remove silks from fresh corn, then wash. On a large square of foil, brush each ear with softened butter. Pour about 2 or 3 tablespoons sauce over each ear. Carefully close foil to cover and seal. Place on grill and cook for about 20 minutes, turning often.

182

· INDEX ·

A

183